Love Absolute

♥HeleneMarie♥

Copyright © 2016 ♥HeleneMarie♥
All rights reserved.

www.HeleneMarie.com

ISBN:1537352199
ISBN-13: 978-1537352190

About the Author:

HeleneMarie is a dedicated Love Activist; Truth Devotee, Straight-Talker, Spiritually Conscious Path Wanderer, Human Rights & Gender Equality Votary, Life Explorer, Science Venerator, Eco Enthusiast, Writer, Holistic Therapist, Visionary Artist, Aspiring Human Being, Woman.

Contents

Introduction – An Invitation to turn up the Volume on Love

1. I believe in Love 18
2. To Non-Duality and Beyond 22
3. My Story – In The Beginning 32
4. On the Road to Healing 43
5. Facing Belief Head On 62
6. Are you Following your Heart or your Hope? 71
7. Revealing Love 76
8. The Act of Loving 107
9. The Invitation to turn up the Volume on Love..118

I believe in Love.
I feel Love.
I know Love.
I absolutely know Love. That is all I truly know.
I see that actions based on Love nourish, rebuild and heal our world.
I believe in humanity's capacity, capability, ability and primal desire to Love.
I believe that the very essence of humanity is Love.
It is therefore I believe in the possibility of true Peace.

Introduction - An invitation to Turn Up the Volume on Love

This book has been created with change in mind, and with a heart felt plea to all the Earth Brothers & Earth Sisters, People, Mentshn, Earth Angels, Light-Knights, Wizards, Life Explorers, Goddesses, Light-Workers, Spiritually Conscious Path Wanderers and Seekers of this World: that we make a conscious effort to let go of our old survival tricks and coping mechanisms, which are rooted in our core beliefs, and that we instead try something else to what we have been doing for thousands of years.

We have now evolved enough, we are educated enough, we are strong enough, and our Hearts are certainly more than big enough. We have plenty of scientific research to assist us, to include: Epigenetics (which show us that it is our mental-emotional environment, together with our external environment, that create our mental and physical health), Unified Field - Quantum Mechanics - Quantum Biology (which show us that we are all connected and that we together create our world – which at times is not what it appears to be), Neuroscience, Psychology, and plain observation of human behavior. We have lab based experiments and countless scientifically sound studies carried out by respectable scientists who are committed to presenting science at its best.

When we combine science with common sense, honesty and our desire to Love and Be Loved, we have a strong basis for re-building the world that we have created - to a dimension from where we can Live and Love in, as opposed to merely continuously survive in.

I feel it is now time that we uncover and distil what we, for thousands of years, have perceived as love so that we can reveal Love or even Love Absolute, and perhaps harness our 'Love Particle'. For that, we will not have to smash unsuspecting protons together at the speed of light, thus sending their quarks flying, with a Large Hadron Collider. – All we need is: to fearlessly suspend our 'spiritually correct' and 'culturally correct' doctrine, to include the spiritually correct and culturally correct personas that we have embodied for however long; then descend into the deep catacombs of everything that is our being, accompanied with unlimited compassion for our self and our fellow human being, so that we can uncover our core beliefs and true feelings with unprecedented honesty.

I have chosen aspects of my own life story to illustrate how easy it is to accidentally contribute to creating an anti-love ridden world that will only ever achieve survival. The reason for this choice is not that I have an overwhelming 'urge to purge', or to go on and on about my miserable childhood and anti-love ridden path. The reasoning is simply: 1. That my story is true - and without working from truth we will not be able to change anything at all.

2. That although my life story is unique, the various issues of suffering, caused by anti-love and non-love, are most certainly very common. And some of the factors, such as physical, emotional and sexual abuse, are part of the great many dark and desperately sad statistics characteristic of the world of today. For example, in October, 2014, UNICEF published the following two reports:

United Nations Children's Fund, Hidden in Plain Sight: A statistical analysis of violence against children, UNICEF, New York, 2014, and **A Statistical Snapshot of Violence against Adolescent Girls, UNICEF, New York, 2014**. UNICEF found that around 120 million girls worldwide have experienced forced intercourse or other forced sexual acts at some point in their lives. Boys experience sexual violence too but to a far lesser extent according to available data. I read those two reports with tears streaming; not just because the words cut straight into anybody's heart, but also because I suspect that UNICEF only managed to scratch the surface of this very gruesome iceberg with the data they were able to secure. Every day, boys and girls around the world are abused violently and sexually by their mother, or father, or grand-mother, or grand-father, or brother, or sister, or guardian, or uncle, or aunt, or cousin, or boyfriend, or girlfriend, or family friend, or neighbor, or school mate, or "friend", or vicar, priest, pastor, or teacher, or coach, or doctor, or acquaintance or stranger. And every day, thousands of children are falling through the cracks of society due to incompetence and neglect.

Readers that have spent some time with self-development, New Age and holistic living will recognize many of the processes I have put myself through, and will also be able to find themselves in many of my own life experiences. Readers for whom all of this is new to will probably benefit from knowing that the feelings, experiences and thought patterns described are completely normal, and sometimes necessary, when you embark on a spiritual path based on conscious self-enquiry. It may at first appear as self-absorption at its worst, but the difference between 'normal people' who do not seek to know themselves and 'conscious self-enquiry path wanderers' is that both think about themselves all the time (because we constantly have to refer back to our self in order to make sense of everything we are thinking and experiencing) – it is just the conscious self-enquiry path wanderers who get to know themselves to such a degree that they are able to take ultimate responsibility for their own thoughts and subsequent actions.

I hope you will find it interesting and even funny in places, which is entirely deliberate, as I have come across and participated in a fair amount of spiritual BS in my life. You should also be able to draw parallels between the New Age and holistic concepts and the belief systems that are founded in atheism as well as common world religions – we are all, after all, mere human beings.

My motives behind writing this book are really quite selfish: For over 20 years I strived to not take anything personally. I strived to believe that 'everything that happens is meant to be' (the version of this belief for other world religions would be:

'Everything that happens is God's will'), 'all is well', 'everything that happens is perfect - including suffering', and 'suffering only exist if we believe our own thoughts of suffering'. I wanted to believe that on the basis that everything that happens is perfect or simply 'just is', we should just practice mindfulness, live in the now, accept 'what is', 'let it be', 'be with it', 'let it go', 'transform suffering within', and let others be and believe what they choose - all belonging to a popular belief system created by well-meaning Non-Dualists thousands of years ago. I so wanted to master this belief system as I believed that as it would result in 'inner peace' that it could heal our world including myself. This belief was also supported by 'adult logic' that a lot of us adopt when we let go of our childhood wisdom. This logic is founded in a mixture of three beliefs: 1. That we do not have, or have to have, the emotional capacity necessary to deal with the suffering that other people experience around us. 2. That our warped interpretation of Charles Darwin's work in respect of 'the survival of the fittest' combined with our propensity to comparing us humans with other mammals - mammals that are governed by brutal pecking order and that are forced to kill in order to live, serve as valid scientific explanation of human behavior. 3. That one of the main purposes for being a human being is to learn – and you learn the most valuable lessons from suffering and hardship.

This has resulted in the stance that it is simply human nature to cause other humans suffering in order to learn, survive and make our way in the world. And so we hear the statement, "Well, what do you expect with that many people trying to live together on one small planet – we are bound to clash, and fight, and hurt and kill".

Then not so long ago, I realized that although this type of belief system and concept living does help our own little personal world short term, as it does help us cope, it will keep real suffering, caused by anti-love and non-love, to continuously manifest in the world that we all share. At this point, my dear old pals, the non-dualists and spiritually and scientifically correct doctrine thinkers, would jump in reminding us all that the world that we share is an illusion, and that we in reality do not experience the same world. So just to clarify that the world that I am referring to is this one:

It is the world that currently has exceeded a population of 7 billion people. It is the world that creates Presidents and Prime Ministers and we are, at the time of writing, still waiting for the people of various countries to create their own peoples' revolution so that they can prize the dictators off their super-glued reigns. It is the world that has credit cards, household bills, school runs, football, soccer, television, pollution, health insurance, corruption, art, raves, gigs, concerts, birthday parties, weddings and funerals. It is also the world that continuously sends their young men and women to war, in order to protect the business interests of the oil and weapon's industry, under the pretence that your country is in danger; then welcome them home - physically and emotionally mutilated. It is the world that has children living on the streets. It is the world that has rape, slavery, murder, child soldiers, abuse and bullying. It is the world that has the most exquisite flora and fauna imaginable; it is the world that has animal and plant species disappearing faster than we can identify any undiscovered. It is in this world where our 'adult logic' and spiritually and culturally correct doctrine (whatever line of chosen faith or belief system) is just enabling us to create more of the same old destruction and suffering - and has been for thousands of years. So now, I refuse to settle with inner peace. Now, I take suffering personally. I take World Peace personally. I take Love personally. And I am now inviting you, my fellow Earth Brother and Earth Sister, to examine your core belief system together with the phenomena we call Love. We have to examine our core belief system, as it is fuelling all our thoughts and feelings. And it is our thoughts and feelings that are essentially creating our world.

But please do not be afraid, I am not suggesting that you stop believing in God or that you relinquish your chosen faith or belief system - whether you are a Christian, Jew, Muslim, Buddhist, Agnostic, Atheist or subscribe to any other religious or scientific spiritual identity. I am simply asking that you find a way of living your spiritual identity whilst considering letting go of your belief in the necessity of suffering.

The thing is, I have had to succumb to my truth and this truth is: that all is and never will be well in my world as long as other people are suffering. And I would like to ask for your help in the hope that you really feel this same truth, and that you will find the benefits of creating a loving world more attractive than sustaining the anti-love ridden world that we have created. Then I would like to invite you to join me in turning up the volume of Love.

Ground Rules

The ground rules that I live by and therefore write by are based on the following knowledge:

- ♥ Every human being is born equal: No human being has more right to being alive and enjoying the benefits of our society than anybody else. If you are a heterosexual, lesbian, gay, bisexual, or asexual woman, man, girl, boy or gender-neutral, whether born with a corresponding body or having to transition – to put it simply, if you are residing in a Homo sapiens body - then you are a completely natural human being with an equal right to claim your happy space on Planet Earth. Sadly, as masters of anti-love and non-love, human kind has created a world that does not provide, and often deliberately prevent, equal opportunities to fulfill this birth-right.

- ♥ Every human being is born free to create, choose and change their life: Although this is true, not every human being know that they have this freedom - especially if they have been submitted to anti-love and non-love to such a degree that they are not capable of choosing freely until they seek or are offered care and healing assistance.

- No human being is born evil and no human being wants to become evil: Evil/anti-love is generated and cultivated by human beings submitting children to anti-love and non-love. Even neuro-scientists agree that factors such as excess testosterone, low level pre-frontal cortex activity and the effects of the MAOA gene (the Warrior Gene) do not alone produce sociopaths and psychopaths; environmental factors such as child abuse, neglect, negative socialization as well as substance abuse, caused by same, all play the deciding blow in forming any human being's evil beliefs and subsequent callus and evil actions. Based on Epigenetics, I go further and state that it is incompetence, neglect, child abuse and negative socialization that create excess testosterone, low pre-frontal cortex activity and the occurrence of the MAOA gene.

- Every human being (including grossly incompetent parents, paedophiles, terrorists and dictators) always do their best: We are always able to do better, and do good instead of evil, but it is our emotional development and subsequent emotional state, at any given moment, which renders us either capable or incapable of doing better and doing good.

- No human being, alive in this world today, has had a truly happy, love filled and harmonious childhood: If you, by some miracle, have not experienced anti-love and non-love on your own body and mind - you will have witnessed it.

- ♥ Every human being is born loveable: Loving and being loved is our birth-right. We are all lovable. You are lovable. I am loveable. Always have been. Always will be. We are all able to love. It cannot be earned. You don't even have to 'qualify' by learning to love yourself first. It simply comes automatically as part of the packet with being born into this dimension - dimension Earth.

Definition of suffering caused by Anti-Love and Non-Love

Anti-love: Anti-love results in suffering that is created by human beings who cause other people the most terrible, horrific and soul-crushing experiences. Those experiences include: child abuse and neglect, sexual abuse, Female Genital Mutilation, slavery, sex trade and forced prostitution, emotional and mental abuse, rape, assault, murder, torture, genocide, racism, hate crime, gender oppression, bullying etc.

Non-love: Non-love also results in suffering as it is based on one person's desire for another person to fulfill their need. When you get your need fulfilled – you feel good. There is no element of love being shared or exchanged between two people; it is simply an ego-trip of emotional masturbation run by the non-lover so that they can get a fix of feeling good or avoid feeling bad. To ensure success for the non-lover it is therefore, with the aid of subconsciously driven manipulation, often portrayed as love. A non-lover will most often convince themselves that what they are feeling *is* love because it makes them feel good. So this "love" looks like kind, thoughtful, helpful, generous, protective, passionate, caring and grateful gestures while it slowly sucks the life out of the receiver and steadily corrodes the relationship. Non-lovers are not aware of that their feelings and actions have nothing to do with Love.

1. I believe in Love

So, I believe in Love.   Nine times out of ten, when I declare my core belief to people that I meet, they respond like this: "Oh that is not a problem –", or, "Oh, that is ok – ", "- because God is Love anyway". And every time I respond: "Not for me. For me, I believe in Love. Love is Love. God is something else. God is for somebody else".

It is really only very recently when I, at the age of 45, got to the bottom of what I actually believe; what I actually believe in; what I actually know. I had come to the end of my 20+ year path of Non-Duality a couple of years earlier, and it had left me a bit shell-shocked and deflated, and leaving behind this nagging realization: "What in the hollow halls of Hades have I been doing?!" For all those years I could have been contributing much better to a peaceful and loving world, and I had instead buried my head and my heart in the pretty sand of spiritually correct dogma.   But here I was, I had now fallen out of the other end of Non-Duality, and I was starring into the neon-lit fact that Non-Duality was after all nothing else than yet another type of concept living - a type of concept living aiming to be 'one' but only achieving to be 'one step ahead' of suffering. And so I took upon myself to lay down the last and very elaborate thought tools that had supported this belief and kept it afloat for all of those years.

The most elaborate, lovingly carved and beautifully ornamented tool was my belief in a God concept. It was the very foundation of my carefully thought out survival trick. There it was, as the ultimate fall-back, the ace in my sleeve, and the last get-out clause from giving a 100% commitment to my life and our world. When I looked at it with 100% honesty; as if I had consumed all the truth-serum in the world, I saw that my belief had merely been a hope. I had needed to hope that when I was too exhausted to carry on, that there was God who would pick me up and carry me. I had needed to hope that there was divine meaning in all the suffering of this world, and that God would reveal this divine meaning to us all one day. I had needed to hope that when I had suffered long enough and learnt all my lessons of this life, past and future lives, that God would eventually bestow me that sweet tasting grace. I had needed to hope that, as nobody had been able to love me, that God at least loved me unconditionally. And in spite of simultaneously believing that we are all God (based on the notion that our soul is divine and always a part of God), and that God is simply Source, the Universe, Life, a Universal Force or Entity, I was hoping, deep down, that there was this additional side to God: that God was keeping an eye on us, and who was a deciding factor in the soul-contracts of our lives, and who would hear our prayers and provide ultimate and sacred meaning to staying alive.

When I looked at these revelations with pure honesty, I saw that what I had believed was something I had actually hoped. I had not 'believed in God'; I had 'hoped in God'. With the same level of honesty I could see that I did not believe in Angels; I 'wanted to believe' in Angels. I wanted to believe because it gave me hope.

Hope is great. When everything fails and all is lost – there is always hope. Even when we lose faith – there is hope. Hope keeps us going and it keeps us alive. There is nothing wrong with hope when we want to survive. But hope cannot achieve much more than that and the danger with striving for hope and settling with hope is that, if we follow our hope we cannot follow our Heart.

My God concept had been based loosely on positive aspects of the Christian and Buddhist belief systems. But in spite of the aspects of those major religions I could no longer fit myself into either of those God concepts. The word itself, God, spoken and abused to and for death by human kind was rendered meaningless. I even asked myself: "So, the God that I do not believe in does not exist – but what if there is a God, or God concept, that I *can believe in* that *therefore can exist*?" Nothing happened. Nothing appeared. Just nothing. A few days passed. To be more exact, a few very distressing days passed. How would I be able to carry on without having a God concept to hang on to? How would I be able to manage without having God to keep an eye on me, covering my back and willing me on to staying alive? What did I have left if I did not have God? Was life even possible without God? But then, the distress started to ease. Then ease some more. Then it seemed to softly fall away until it had evaporated and left my being altogether. And when I saw that I was still here - together with the millions of agnostics and atheists that do not believe in a God concept - and I realized that nothing had actually changed for the worse, something started to happen - a quiet emergence of Love. With tears streaming, I suddenly but gently knew that not only did I believe in Love, I knew Love – I absolutely knew Love. I knew Love in my entire being and I knew Love in the entire world. Just Love. Just pure undiluted Love. Nothing else claiming to be Love. Nothing else containing Love. Nothing else mixed with Love. Nothing else masked as Love. Nothing else mistaken for Love. Love in its purest form. Love Absolute.

I now knew, with effortless, unwavering and liberating certainty that - I know Love. That is all I truly know.

What do you want to believe in?

What do you 'hope in'?

What do you know?

2. To Non-Duality and Beyond

The basic Non-Duality belief concept subscribe to the following notion – hold on to your halo whilst slowly reading the following: That we are the awareness of consciousness observing itself. This entails that everything just 'is' and we just 'are'. Everything just is awareness; we just are awareness. We do not suffer, as suffering is not suffering but just a divinely intelligent event that 'is'; together with everything else that just 'is'. Instead what we in 'reality' do is that we **observe thoughts** about suffering, and the only thing that goes wrong and breaks our inner peace is when we **believe** the thoughts we observe about suffering. So it is therefore **our judgment** that something is painful, wrong or evil that makes us suffer – **not the actual event or experience** that we judge as painful, wrong or evil.

Non-Duality springs from religions such as Buddhism, Hinduism, Taoism and Vedanta and there are many paths and aspects of how we have adopted Non-Duality in to our spiritually conscious lives: In the one bleak end of the spectrum we can perceive our World as a mere 'expression' of events that cannot be defined, matter including human form cannot be defined, and human interaction and communication is deemed meaningless movements and sounds that cannot be defined either. At the other more optimistic end of the spectrum we perceive our World as perfect 'as it is' and so it just 'is', and every action and occurrence we experience, including suffering, similarly just 'is' as well – we do not judge it as good or bad – it just 'is' in every divinely perfect moment.

The following statements are often used when describing Non-Duality:

"Full acceptance of every moment"

"Living without judgment and resistance to life"

"Pure being in every now"

"Surrendering to every now"

"The World and Life is perfect and beautiful. Every experience is perfect and beautiful. Happiness is perfect and beautiful. Pain and suffering is perfect and beautiful"

"The empirical worldview is an illusion/is un-real"

"It only exists if it exists in you (in your mind)"

"Being you - without your story"

"Life is an expression of the Divine. The world just is"

"Absolute Oneness – we are God and God is us" - as opposed to God versus Human Being

The foregoing statements may come across as pure crazy-talk or utter woo-woo, but the essence of non-duality has been translated into the language of mere mortals. To name a few, Non-Duality has been promoted in the western world by highly respected authors and facilitators such as Eckhart Tolle (he wrote 'A New Earth'), Byron Katie (she wrote 'Loving What Is'), Helen Schuman and William Thetford (they wrote 'A Course in Miracles'). We will all have come across the basic aspects, that everything 'just is' or 'is perfect' and 'living without judgment or resistance to life', when Louise Hay taught us to say, "All is well in my World"; when Richard Carlson taught us, "Don't sweat the small stuff"; and when John Lennon sang "Let it Be". And it has, over the past few decades, become increasingly popular to 'go with the flow' and to adopt 'mindfulness' in to our daily lives as well.

The path of Non-Duality has funnily enough a dual potential: to either fully immerse yourself in life, or to fully escape from life.

The experience of Non-Duality is usually achieved via meditation aiming for a state of pure awareness, together with continued self enquiry into our own belief and experience about life – what we think it is, who we think we are, who we really are, what is really happening, what is really true, and the goal is most often to simply 'be awareness' as much as possible until this is achieved continuously and thereby mastered.

I have practiced self enquiry on a daily basis for many years, and by switching between observing my thoughts and questioning everything that I thought and felt, I have helped myself gain useful insight into the power of how our thoughts shape our world. Self enquiry can be as simple as asking yourself: "What is in reality really happening right now?", "What am I actually doing/being right now?" Those two questions can be really helpful when you are in the midst of sweating the small stuff, such as panicking because traffic is causing you to be late for work, or if you have one of those 'we are all going to die moments' because your most important client has decided to go elsewhere. Another good question can be: "So how is this really working for me?" I used that particular question when I realized that, for the majority of my life, I had stuck to two big contradictory core beliefs: "So, in order to cope with the suffering in my life, I chose to believe that suffering is simply always 'meant to be' and is an important ingredient in anybody's life in order to learn lessons and develop our soul on our Karma spiral; at the same time I also desperately want to believe in the possibility of World Peace and the eradication of all suffering? So…, how is that working for me?" "Uh oh!….." I saw that both beliefs were my creation, and that I had chosen one belief based on my need to find meaning in the suffering I had and was experiencing in order to cope and survive; and I had chosen another belief based on wanting to follow my heart. When I put that together with the fact that it is our beliefs that create our world – I decided that I would rather believe in World Peace than the necessity of suffering.

To explore a deeper level of Non-Duality, an enquiry session, or enquiry meditation, could go like this: I ask myself; "Who am I?" and the following answers could come up: I am HeleneMarie → I am a woman → I am a human being → I am a soul → I am God (because my soul is divine and a part of God) → I am Peace → I am Love → I am no-thing → I am every-thing → I am → I am awareness → I am consciousness → I am the awareness of consciousness/I am the awareness of consciousness observing itself. Being awareness, or being the awareness of consciousness observing itself, is something I have experienced through meditation in different ways: One experience has been an awareness of being no-thing but still with a sense of self (the 'I Am') = I am no-thing. Another experience has been a sense of being everything accompanied by the experience of altruism and a sense of the self being a Universal self, and without the I Am but rather a We Are One. Another experience has been being awareness without a sense of nothing, of everything or anybody, and without being loaded with a self of any kind. The only thing that holds on to a self is when I interrupt the experience with my thinking with the knowledge that I was experiencing this because I am alive in a human body.

To put it mildly, those experiences are simply A-MA-ZING and it can feel like an other-worldly and blissfully divine experience most times. You can also keep the experience going in your day to day life by recalling the blissful meditation experience and mixing it with the conclusion from your self enquiry, reminding yourself that you are awareness no matter what is happening in your life. The danger with this though is, that some people decide to draw the conclusion that this is the only real and true reality and that everything else that is happening in our world is an illusion. And so they do everything they can to hold on to their experience, and ensure that their feeling of bliss is not short-lived. And for that they need to re-name suffering to something that 'just is' thus endorsing suffering as a valid ingredient, on par with love and happiness, in everybody's lives. This is just another way that we can add to all our other directions of belief systems that we have invented for coping with the world that we have all created.

We also have the propensity to dissect how our brain and body works, as well as shrinking our world to subatomic levels – usually in our noble quest to uncover what consciousness actually is. But instead of utilizing this mind-lifting knowledge to reveal how we create our physical lives in this world, there has been a tendency to concluding that it proves that our world does not really exist but that it is simply our senses that create an experience of a world in any given moment in time; time that does not exist either. This is of course also true at some level but it is rather close to creating the full circle and returning to the outdated stance that we are mere biological machines.

I know that we can do much, much better than this and I think we should aim much, much higher.

I have had countless moments of either experiencing the blissful state of 'being awareness' or just 'being One' and in the next moment brutally dragged into the undeniable fact that I am a completely normal human being with basic needs. One such typical instance that springs to mind is one pleasant sunny morning when I was driving to London. I had been driving for a couple of hours listening to Deva Premal & Miten and singing along to Om Namo Bhagavate, on repeat, and I was feeling ever so serene and ever so altruistic. I was just One with the world and everything was perfect, and I loved every single being on this beautiful planet. As always, I had to stop at the traffic lights where Baker Street crosses Marylebone Road, and within seconds a grubby looking man appeared right next to the driver's side window and proceeded to clean my windscreen. In a split second I was overcome with extreme fright - equal to the scene in "I Am Legend" where Will Smith's character is standing in his laboratory behind a bullet-proof glass wall whilst raging mutants, set on killing and eating him, violently and successfully break down the glass wall with relentless determination – let alone a middle aged man armed with a sponge and a squeegee. I managed to get him to leave by shouting "NO!" whilst thinking, "get the hell away from me" combined with a meek "heeellllp!", and indicating I was releasing my seatbelt and about to open the door. After he had left, I proceeded to shake and laugh hysterically whilst feeling embarrassed from being so frightened. Two hours of bliss had evaporated in a split second and replaced by my basic need to feel safe. Altruism, serenity and oneness was aaaaall gone and I most definitely did not feel any love for the squeegee man.

I can certainly understand that some people prefer to stay in the blissful state of being awareness, especially if they are struggling in this world that we have created. Then 'being what it is, that is the essence of you, but without your past story, and without your memories and future hopes and fears', can be a tremendous relief. It has often helped me when being a human being no longer made sense to me. - When I felt that I had nothing to lose and when I was so tired, and used up, and exhausted from physical pain that I did not care if I was dead or alive; when I did not care what I had or did not have; when the World 'just was' with or without me and with or without you my fellow human being. In those times the Non-Duality concept gave me a sense of being in a safe-house, protecting me from having to deal with all the horror moments of the world and protecting me from feeling complete despair and helplessness – I 'just was' and it was neither good or bad, and everybody else 'just were' and that was neither good or bad, no matter what they were going through.

For me, self enquiry started when I was about 12 years old, when life presented me with teen parties and the preparation for my Christian Confirmation. I found those teenage-angst ridden parties utterly pointless, and after trying it out I decided to spare myself from the sheer boredom and instead question what it was that my class mates got out of it that I did not, as we were clearly not experiencing the same thing. Similarly with the preparation for my Christian Confirmation I found that I did not fit in with this doctrine, which was apparently true for so many and adhered to by so many, and that I would be lying if I went through with it. And so I started to question everything - including myself. For the record, I did go through with my Confirmation to avoid making my biological mother angry, as well as ensuring that I got to wear a white dress from Laura Ashley, and that I got all my Confirmation presents.

There are many benefits associated with self enquiry, for example:

It does wonders for hoicking you back when your monkey-mind has gone walkabouts or run-arounds, and so it shouts, "Oy you, get back here! Get back right here in the now, as in right now!"

It helps reveal how we often treat people, as well as ourselves, in ways that we hold other people responsible for in doing to us.

It is brilliant for your unplanned trips to the land of endless worry, where you suddenly find yourself playing out worst case scenarios to include potential natural disasters, made up nasty people and continuous bad luck, and so it pulls you out of all those disappointments that will never come true.

It is great for dispelling the myths we were brought up to believe, and it frees us from religious suppression associated with some religious institutions. I am God, God is Me, We are One - help us to withdraw from the thunder of institutional disapproval and we are no longer miserable sinners and good-for-nothing human beings.

It spares you from playing all the horror movies of your past, when it reminds you every time you go to that specific cinema that the rule is: No repeat screenings!

It assists you in withdrawing from the belief that you are a victim and it is a super tool for 'stop sweating the small stuff'. So, self enquiry in itself is a very useful tool that I can recommend highly when life calls us to cope short term.

The biggest and most important benefit is though, that if you use self enquiry to get to the truth about yourself and to really know yourself; to really know what you are thinking and feeling and what is motivating you in every moment of the day - you reach a point of no return where you lose the ability to BS (bullshit) yourself: Every time you want to fabricate a story about your thoughts and feelings in any given moment, for example pretend that your intentions are purely altruistic, or you are tempted to blame somebody else for your own self-inflicted misery, the lie is so wholly uncomfortable that you quickly, and often in a split second, revert to the truth.

3. My Story – In the Beginning

I, like so many of us, had what I call a Cortisol-Childhood – in other words, a VERY STRESSFUL childhood, and it was a continuously stressful childhood that was riddled with abuse and fear. Those who were meant to care for me - didn't. Those who were meant to be kind to me – wasn't. Those who were meant to protect me – didn't. Those who supposedly loved me – certainly had a "funny way" of showing it. Not a day passed where I was not afraid or terrified, either during the whole day or some of the day. I did not know that I had the right to defend myself, protect myself, say NO or run away - that was frightened out of me from an early age. So as I could not honour my natural 'fight or flight' response, I had to adopt the method of befriending and pleasing my tormentors (a survival mechanism known as compliance). My childhood taught me that I was completely worthless and unlovable but useful to satisfy the needs of others, and this is what I brought with me into my adult life.

I was born into a family that never stood a chance of succeeding. I will not go into all the horrible factors or soul-crushing details for the following reasons:

1. I would not be able to describe some of my experiences as I feel that I would contaminate perfectly good words by utilizing them to create the sentences required to describing those experiences. And I need those words for creating other sentences. 2. I feel that detailed personal misery have become a reliable ingredient in the entertainment industry, and whilst it sometimes serve as an important source of information for fellow survivors - it also becomes a gory misery ridden and stress inducing fix for misery addicts, and I now value myself enough to refrain from becoming somebody's fix. 3. It basically does not take a lot of explanation to illustrate why our family never stood a chance, and what the core anti-love force was behind the main reason I became to believe that I was utterly worthless and unlovable:

The main reason was that my biological mother's father was a paedophile. He had abused my biological mother since she was a little girl. She had had a grossly incompetent mother who was deemed degraded and useless as a woman by her paedophile husband after a full hysterectomy, and she had encouraged her daughter with: "Are you sleeping with Dad tonight?" He had brainwashed his daughter into believing that she was the most special girl in his life, and that his "special treatment" of her was because he loved her more than anything and anybody else in the whole world. He had destroyed her so thoroughly that she saw nothing wrong with keeping him close in her adult life. And when she had my two year older sister and later me, she saw no reason to keep us safe from him.

When my biological mother divorced from my Dad, she moved back to the area where her paedophile father lived, and he was now only a short walk away. He would then come for dinner every Sunday, some times he would stay the night, and she also invited him along on holidays where he would share a room with my sister and me. Should she ever have had the slightest train of thoughts relating to if keeping her children safe from her paedophile father was a good idea or not, then she had an excellent opportunity to make up her mind at one of those holidays:

It was bedtime and her two little daughters, approximately 8 and 10 years old, had to share a bedroom with her paedophile father. There was 1 double bed and 1 single bed in the room. She had gone to bed in the room across the hall with her boyfriend (my dear Step Dad – a decent and caring man who had no idea what was going on). Her two daughters got into an argument with her paedophile father when he insisted that he wanted to share the double bed with one of her daughters. Her daughters kept on insisting that he slept in the single bed and that her two daughters shared the double bed. Her paedophile father would not give in and this resulted in increasingly raised voices. In the end, the argument had become so loud that she could hear it across the hall and she came into the room and asked angrily what was going on. Her two distraught daughters explained that he refused to sleep in the single bed and that none of them wanted to share the double bed with him. She told her paedophile father that he had to sleep in the single bed. He refused. She then decided that her eldest daughter should be the one that should share the double bed with her paedophile father. Her eldest daughter was angry about this decision. She then went right up close and threatened her paedophile father with …….

her index finger...... and said: "You are not going to do anything?!" He answered, "No nooo". She then left her two daughters with her paedophile father and went to bed in the bedroom across the hall. Her two daughters went to bed and so did her paedophile father. I was lying in the single bed. I felt so terrified and so relieved, and so guilty that I had been spared. I felt so afraid of what the consequences would be because I had been spared – did this mean that it would be "my turn" the next day? I then heard that my biological mother's paedophile father asked my sister to tickle his back. My strong and brave sister, who knew she had the right to say no shouted: "NO!", and she positioned herself at the very edge of the double bed away from him. He was astonished and did not try to approach her again. I fainted in to sleep. The next morning I woke up by my biological mother's paedophile father standing in his underwear starring at me. I deferentially said: "Good morning Granddad". And he replied, "Good morning".

That day we moved to another hotel where we had to share a room with him again. It was a much larger room with one single bed in one end of the room and the double bed in the other end. I had a tight knot in my stomach all day from terror and dread. And so I was so relieved to discover that, without any discussion at all, it had been decided that he had to use the single bed.

That evening my strong and brave sister saved me from being stung by a dark brown scorpion. We had gone to bed and she noticed something on my leg and shouted: "It's a scorpion!" Within a split second I found myself standing on a chair whilst my strong and brave sister pulled out the beds and caught the scorpion in a chocolate box.

My sister also saved me from dying from carbon monoxide poisoning: We would visit our Dad every fortnight and every visit would finish with our Dad stressed, grumpy and often angry, driving us directly to school very early on the Monday morning. Just like his pilot check list those mornings would enfold the same every time: woken up early, shower, breakfast, pack your things, Dad opens the garage door and starts the car, Dad shouts: "Kids, get in the car!", we get into the basement which has a door leading out to the double garage, pass the basement bathroom where Dad is combing his hair, we get into the car, Dad checks that all the doors are locked upstairs and gets into the car ca. two minutes later, drives us out, stops the car to shut and lock the garage door, drives off. This time was different. There was a towel in front of the door leading out to the garage, which was allegedly to stop the draft. We had been given the order to get in the car but the garage door was closed even though the engine was running. Our Dad told us to keep the car doors open and then left the garage. My sister and I sat in the back seat of the car for ages and ages and we were starting to feel sick. We looked at each other and confirmed that we both felt the same. My strong and brave sister then got out of the car, unlocked the garage door, pulled it up as far as she could and then jumped as high as she could so that she could catch the little rope to pull the heavy garage door all the way back, then she got back into the car. I was afraid that our Dad would get really angry about this. We then sat in the car, again for ages and ages, until our Dad finally opened the door. And instead of opening it fast and closing it behind him, he opened it slowly and peeked out with the kind of expression you have on your face when you are dreading what you might find. He had a piece of paper in his hand. He discovered that the garage door was open and asked who had done that. My sister owned up to it immediately and he said, "oh". He then said he just had to do something and then we would be leaving. He came back about 10 minutes later and he looked like he had been vomiting. He then got in the car and put a menthol pastille in his mouth that he would usually take together with a cigarette. We then drove to school. My Dad was in a real dark place at the time and he was some times mentioning suicide when he spoke to his Mum, my nice Grandmother, and each time she would remind him that he had his two precious daughters to live for. My guess is that he was planning to kill us all three, himself being helped along with a handful of sleeping tablets, and leave a heart breaking note behind. I will never know for sure of course.

As you can imagine, my biological mother had to have some kind of outlet from everything she was suppressing, and this was facilitated by her regular rages over everything that her two daughters "did wrong". So my sister and I would get beaten if we were being too noisy, if we had not finished cleaning the house in time for when she returned from her part time job as a music teacher, and especially if we had forgotten to wipe the skirting boards behind the beds. We were also submitted to occasional experiences akin to the 'no wire-hangers!' scene from the film, 'Mommie Dearest' (a film based on Christine Crawford's biography - check it out on Youtube). My biological mother was exceedingly strong and built with very manly muscular arms, and when she hit her children she did it with great enthusiasm and without holding back in the slightest.

I should clarify that I refer to my parents as 'my biological mother' and 'my Dad': My 'biological mother', because she was not capable of being kind, caring and taking a loving interest in her children like a Mum; and her gross incompetence and regular violent physical and emotional abuse prevented her from fulfilling the basic skills, such as bringing up her children in a safe and loving environment, that a Mother would have. But she did give birth to me so she is my biological mother. My 'Dad', because he was more 'innocent' in his incompetence compared to my biological mother, and he did manage to bring forth his kind and gentle soul on occasion. He even told me, before his body gave up at the age of 57 because of the damage caused by alcohol, that he loved me and that he was so very sorry if he was to blame for my physical suffering. I also strongly suspect that there is a smidgen of my need to have had at least one parent that wasn't too bad - based on the possibility that a part of me cannot cope with the thought of not having had any proper parents at all, and so it feels better to have had a 'Dad'. The foregoing may come across as somewhat cynical, indulgent or demonstrative but please be assured that there is none intended – it is simply my honest solution to being able to refer to my parents.

My Dad's alcohol addiction became obvious when he and my biological mother divorced. He was a pilot – a damn good pilot – similarly to the Maverick character in the film, 'Top Gun'. But one of the various crosses he had had to bear from birth was that his elder brother, Flemming, had died from pneumonia at the age of two, a few years before my

Dad was born. He was never able to live up to this perfect little boy; this perfect little pretty boy with golden curly hair; this perfect little pretty and happy boy; this perfect little pretty, happy and beloved boy, and so my Dad started to self-sabotage his life with alcohol at a time when his little daughters needed him the most. He was a gentle soul with a quirky sense of humor - attractive too in his Captain's uniform with 4 gold stripes on the shoulders and cuffs. Unfortunately he was of the opinion that it was completely acceptable to subscribe to porn magazines and have them scattered around the house, and so I did unfortunately grow up with the stereotypical male chauvinistic view: that female pornography and prostitution is just natural ingredient of our world. He had thankfully met a lovely airhostess that moved in with him when I was five years old. Her name is Rikke. Rikke can remember when my Dad told her, during an around the world flight, that I had just been born. Rikke is one of the reasons I am still here. The other reasons are my Dad's Mum, Emmy Magdalene (she cared about me), my Dad's neighbor, Bodil (she encouraged my creativity), and I think there is an additional reason: that we are brought in to this dimension, all carrying the knowledge of Love; as if we are all carrying around a tiny but almighty particle, a Love Particle, that reminds us of pure Love. It reminds us that Love is possible and always available to us in this Dimension Earth. And so we hang on to this knowledge as if the Universe had thrown out survival ropes for us to hang on to for as long as we manage to hold on to this knowledge. And we continue to hang on even when it becomes merely a distant memory. Rikke simply welcomed me in to her open arms and heart. She cared for me and she was always happy to see me. She hugged me with bountiful care, and she was the only adult person that I was never afraid of. I felt safe when she was there. And so I got to experience the feeling of being momentarily safe and cared for every fortnight when my sister and I were visiting our Dad and Rikke. After several years of trying, Rikke eventually had no choice but to leave my Dad due to his drinking.

It took me many, many years to understand that alcoholism is a real physical illness where the body is so addicted to alcohol that every cell in the body is screaming for it whenever the sufferer is trying to stop. I couldn't understand why he didn't just stop, and I drew the conclusion that he didn't have any will power and just didn't want to stop. It is of course the same as saying to a cancer sufferer: "Why don't you just stop having cancer?!" The alcoholic as well as the cancer sufferer do not like to be ill and do not want to be ill but they both need expert help to get better.

As with a lot of children going through harrowing times, I looked like a completely normal, happy and obedient child. I did my home work, was creative and had several friends that I played with after school. My life also looked normal and most would agree that I seemed to have a nice and comfortable life as a typical Scandinavian girl in the 70 and 80'ies. I had my own room with good furniture. I had birthday parties and always got nice presents for birthdays and Christmas. My biological mother used to read bed-time stories and sing lullabies to me when I was little. I had piano lessons, and I was supported for being creative. In my early teens however, it became increasingly difficult for me to cope and so I became more withdrawn, pensive and defensive. This was interpreted by my family as that I was cold and cynical. My body eventually started to react and I got ill. I developed all the symptoms associated with Polycystic Ovarian Syndrome (PCOS) to include weight gain, abnormal hair growth, cystic acne and lethargy. I also started to suffer from debilitating hormonal migraines*. I became the freak in the high school that I was attending, and regular humiliation combined with the heavy load of school work, and having to work after school to pay for staying at home, resulted in yet further increased stress levels.

*Unless you suffer from migraines then of course you can't guess what a migraine is. Most people are of the understanding that a migraine is just a strong headache so I think I should clarify how my migraines crippled my life: The attacks last between 1 and 3 days (on occasion up to 5 days) with the following symptoms: melatonin and serotonin imbalance that causes a desperate need for the body to sleep but you can't because of pain and vomiting, vomiting for 1 to 24 hours; when the vomiting starts to get hold it happens every 5 to 10 minutes for up to 4 hours and then recedes slowly, seeing flashing lights with eyes closed, unable to tolerate any kind of lighting source and flashing or animated lights, unable to cope with watching repetitive and fast movements whether it be people or things, hammering electric pain in part of head or entire head, brain shutting down (one 'circuit' after another) so that I can eventually read words but not understand the meaning. It basically feels like (without exaggerating) having a stroke combined with food poisoning whilst being hit by an electrified hammer on the head once a second. You are essentially being tortured by your own body and there is nothing you can do about it. It then also takes a long time, about a week, to recover after each torture session. When the attacks were at their worst I would have about 2 good days a month, and trying to work full time at the same time was pure hell. Some of my fellow migraineurs have similar attacks, some have lighter attacks, some have even worse attacks and some have other symptoms as well.

4. On the Road to Healing

Over the years I have tried many weird and wonderful tools in my quest to cope with my physical (hormonal imbalance and violent migraines) and emotional (reoccurrence of detailed memories) suffering. I have tried chiropractic therapy, physiotherapy, cranio sacral therapy, NLP, EFT (Tapping), Hypnosis therapy (Hypnotherapy), Chinese Medicine, diet, fasting, Homeopathy, Anthroposophical medicine, Regression, Re-birthing, Kinesiology, Reflexology, Reiki Healing and various other alternative medicine and releasing and healing techniques. Some had absolutely no effect whatsoever and some gave me some temporary relief accompanied by the feeling of moving to a new level of understanding as well as carrying me through a rough patch.

Some of the therapists were excellent and some were completely incompetent where I found it rather worrying that they would be practicing on really vulnerable people as well. The latest example of this was when I wanted to try hypnotherapy as an experiment to see if I could get help with communicating with the subconscious part of my mind, and convince it that I didn't need or want the migraine attacks to occur. The first hypno-therapist had the preconception that migraine occurs in people that are particularly anxious. When she offered this explanation to me I felt that I had just been bombed back to Freudian times where women were looked upon as suffering a lot from Hysteria. I informed her that I thankfully did not suffer with anxiety as I, after working with myself for over 20 years, had analyzed, felt and reacted to every evil act that I had experienced, and that I had turned every trauma stone to the point of boredom. And so I did not suppress anything that could result in anxiety. She then reacted with the outdated psychotherapy stance that if your client resists something then that means automatically that it is because they do not want to face it. I informed her that that stance did not apply to me and we agreed to disagree. But then I would hear, during the hypnosis, that she would tell me that I could safely let go of my anxiety as it was no longer necessary to feel anxious etc. And so I had to concede that she was not capable of helping me. The next hypno-therapist thought that his Anglican Christian belief system was much better than mine and that he would be helping me if he incorporated his beliefs and telling me that I should not spend so much time on thinking about Buddhism and Non-Duality, and combining this with peculiar judgmental stories about his other clients, again during hypnosis. I am always happy to hear about and discuss other people's beliefs but being told what to believe during hypnosis, and without my consent, is of course absolutely unacceptable. I was horrified. I then found a professional and competent hypnotherapist that could clear out all the mental garbage the previous two had left behind.

I myself had my moments of incompetence when I started out as a holistic therapist about 30 years ago. I had been taught to read bodies, and one preconception was that women who have excess body fat on their thighs and upper arms carry around a lot of pent up anger. And so as soon as I got a client with big thighs and upper arms I would apply my preconceived assumption that she was probably were angry indeed. It took me a couple of years to realize that I myself was carrying around a lot of pent up anger but I did not have any excess body fat on my thighs and arms – Uh oh! And so I learned to listen to my clients instead.   I also became preoccupied with wanting super powers to cure people. That was because I found that I was able to remove physical pain from my clients. I would simply lay my hands on the area that was hurting and the pain would disappear within a few minutes. As I found the gratitude and amazement very rewarding, I wanted more of it. I so wanted to 'be allowed' to be able to cure people of their ailments as well. And so I sadly sabotaged my own work when I could have achieved so much good if I had just gotten out of my own way.

This is a little selection of some of the healing concepts I have tried:

Reincarnation and Past Lives:

The idea of past lives was one of my first attempts to understand the big 'why' of my life – why was I suffering so much. I was about 17 when I started reading Raymond Moody's 'Life after Life' and booking my first clairvoyance sessions. I wanted to know what I had done wrong in previous lives so that I could explain why I had been punished so severely in this life. This tied in to my new-found belief in Karma. Until my late twenties I believed that I was being punished in this life due to my actions in a previous life, but this later changed to my belief in Soul Contracts instead: this type of Karma based belief system was more gentle insofar as that you no longer judge yourself or others as possible evil, but that every human being simply need to learn a variety of lessons though experiencing life from a human perspective whatever it may bring and wherever it may place us in society.

None of the clairvoyant mediums could come up with any answers but then I came across two memories of two past lives. The first came about during a past life regression session: I was transported in to a life where I was a six year old girl who lived with my mother and twelve year old brother. I had brown skin and dark brown hair. We lived in a hot country in a village near the sea, and our home consisted of a hut made of red-brown clay, a straw roof and the earth as our floor. Everybody in our village lived in the same type of home – nothing more and nothing less. I was very happy walking home from playing in the warm sea and my mother had made us dinner which consisted of some type of yams mash. My mentally disabled brother suddenly got one of his fits and proceeded to beat me on my head again and again with a heavy wooden log. My head was hurting so so much. Within a minute I was dead. My brother stopped and put down the log. My brother could not help it. He did not know what he was doing. My mother took my dead body and cradled it in her arms and she wept and wept. I started leaving my body quickly and observed my mother from way above how she wept and cradled a little body that had been me. I was no longer in pain. I was just the essence of me.

The second memory came about when a therapist, during a co-creation session, remarked that she saw me in a concentration camp: I was immediately transported to what looked like a poorly equipped gym changing room with tiles on the walls and red worn-down bricks, making them almost soft to tread, on the floor [I am aware that reports note that the floors in the concentration camp gas chambers were made of concrete or cement but the floor I saw was made of red narrow bricks]. My name was Dora and I was deaf. My hair was light blonde, very very thin and unwashed but it was not short like the other women in the room. It was gathered in 2 pig-tails tied with dirty cotton string. I was also not wearing the same grey clothes as the other women. I was wearing a pale yellow – almost beige colored summer dress made of thin cotton voile and I had no shoes on. My body was very pale and extremely skinny. I was so very cold and I could no longer remember how it felt like to feel warm. I had been used by the guards for sex until I had become so ill and riddled with disease that I was no longer useful to them, and it was therefore decided that I should be exterminated. I do not know the other women in the room and they are looking at me as if I am a strange creature. They look worried and some are undressing and some are holding on to their clothes as if somebody had threatened to pull it off their bodies. I am waiting to understand what I am supposed to do. I am hoping that something good is about to happen. I am hoping that I will be allowed a warm shower. Suddenly I smell a horribly nasty smell. The other women start to move around and wave their arms. I stand there on the floor and I cannot feel my feet. Suddenly it hits me – pure evil. Evil on the deepest and darkest level possible. I feel conned and embarrassed that I had thought something good was going to happen. My eyes turn completely black with shock over how evil human beings can be – how evil human beings can choose to be. Then everything goes black. Nothing exists. I no longer exist.

These two snapshots of life feel like the essence of me existing in two other lives before this life. It is however highly likely that those two lives has nothing to do with me. Maybe I picked up somebody else's memories from the ether. As I am fully aware that I am capable of making up a story in a few seconds, it is highly likely that they are two stories I have, subconsciously, made up based on all the real and fictional experiences I have had in this life. Maybe Dora is based on a film I have seen combined with the education I received in my childhood about WW2, and maybe my disabled brother is based on somebody I have heard or read about. I do not know. So the only way I can extract some meaning out of these snapshots is by looking at how they relate to this life. The two memories/stories represent the main strands of this life:

1. That all the people who caused me to suffer cannot help they caused me to suffer as they had experienced suffering themselves or were in some way innocent in their actions.

2. I have often been taken aback and baffled to the bone over why people have attacked me when I had done nothing to hurt them.

3. My upbringing showed me that I was alive so that I could be used by other people to satisfy their needs.

4. I have, at times throughout my life, felt completely paralyzed with chock over how deeply evil human beings can be. For many, many years I felt that I carried a big, round, black, heavy stone around with me, that consisted of all the evil I had come across. I felt that if just the smallest spec was chipped off this stone that it could blow up the entire Universe. In the end I was feeling a constant physical sharp pain in the middle of my Heart Chakra on my back which would just not go away. Thankfully in my early forties I found a great Healer, John McGrath, who helped me heal the pain, and the stone has never been back since.

Loving Yourself

It was through reading 'You can Heal your Life', by Louise Hay, in the late 80'ies, that I came across the term, to love yourself. It had never even crossed my mind that I could love myself. Wouldn't it be so much easier if somebody could just come along and do it for you? I had believed that love was something that I would get from somebody if only I could be perfect enough in their eyes. Unfortunately, in the time that followed I held on to notions that I picked up from various books and teachings that had misunderstood Louise's work, such as 'You will have to learn to love yourself **before** you can love others', and 'you will not be able to receive love **until** you are able to love yourself'. For somebody like me, I immediately took upon myself to learn to love myself because I now believed that I would not be able to give and receive 'proper' love until I had mastered to love myself. I now believed that I had to 'qualify' in order to give and receive love by learning to master self love. A lot of the work in relation to this was positive affirmations. I have to admit that, that technique has never healed anything in my life, and saying to myself that I love myself has never taught me to love myself. I had a friend who would say to herself, several times a day and over a period of over 15 years: "I am healthy, wealthy and happy" – she was none of those things. I have however found that positive affirmations can serve as a very useful mind-shifter when we momentarily need to shift our stagnant thoughts from something negative to something positive.

It took me many, many years until I realized that we are all loveable at all times. There is no universal law that dictates that we are not capable of giving or receiving love until we love our self. If that was the case then very few would receive love in this world. There is however a connection between how we allow others to treat us and the level of worthiness of love we feel for ourselves. The less we feel worthy the more anti-love and non-love we allow in to our lives.

If you do not feel that you love yourself – at least know that you are loveable, now and always.

Mirroring

This concept notes that when we find ourselves in emotional conflict with another person, it is a wake-up call to show us that we ourselves contain the very thing that we dislike in the other person. We are as such reacting because it exists in ourselves. We are seeing ourselves in the other person as if they were a mirror. So for example, if we find another person to be a bully, a complainer or an inconsiderate person, then we can look at our own behavior and see if we in reality do the same to that person or to other people. For example, if I am angry that my partner didn't call me when he could see that he would be running late, then I may discover that I do the same, perhaps not to him though but to my friends. I can then check within why I am behaving like this and then decide to stop that inconsiderate behavior.

Very importantly though, some times you react to that persons behavior because they are mirroring what you believe about yourself. So for example, if you find yourself in a work, friend, or romantic relationship with a bully, then it may be that you are in that relationship because part of you thinks that you do not deserve any better. You are as such actually having a healthy reaction that is trying to tell you to get away from the situation and find healing for the cause of your belief.

Forgiveness

Words are so, so important. I am passionate about words. I feel every corner, curve and edge of every word. I am so grateful for words like and, it, he and she. I am grateful for words like angry, disgusting, unacceptable and nasty. I am grateful for words like beautiful, passionate, delicious and squidgy. I am grateful for yes and I am grateful for no, and I could not imagine a world without words like kind, gentle, soft, light and beloved.

When we need to heal, it is so very important that we use words that we can identify with in order to let go of the feelings we would like to stay in the past, and so that we can live with feelings we want in our present.

Whenever we deal in words we are never far away from some helpful individual who is keen to educate us in the origin of our chosen word and its "real" interpretation – often revealing an outdated interpretation completely alien to our own and fellow human beings' current interpretation. In other instances we are presented with multiple choices of elaborate interpretations when words are just not cutting it. A prime example is forgiveness. Oh how I have tossed, turned and dissected this word for decades in my attempt of trying to adopt it and utilize it in the name of healing. The dictionary notes, Forgive: to pardon, to overlook, to be merciful. If you Google the meaning of forgiveness, you will be presented with hundreds of quotes from famous people, who are trying to give forgiveness an acceptable meaning, and a meaning that is more attractive in order to attempt to apply it, instead of what it actually means – to forgive.

It is a key word that humankind has aspired to for thousands of years because not only does it make you look really good in the eyes of God, it also promises ultimate absolution. You get to decide if the perpetrator deserves your forgiveness. You get to take your power home to yourself again by bestowing forgiveness upon the perpetrator.

Forgiveness has sadly been misused a lot where the victim has forgiven the perpetrator, and then thinks that they have to sustain the same relationship; this being in spite of the perpetrator not changing or healing at all. In my family, this happened when I forgave my biological mother but thought that I should still keep our relationship alive. She continued to be herself and in the end I wasn't able to have a phone call with her without shaking and crying afterwards. It wasn't until I was 28 when I finally found the courage to end our mother-daughter relationship. Thankfully, her reaction was to get absolutely furious and so I knew that I had made the right choice. I also found that I had had too high expectations of what forgiveness would achieve. I was hoping that when you had forgiven a perpetrator that all the bad memories would miraculously disappear. That was of course not the case.

You also see forgiveness misused when communities or entire countries forgive genocide and other atrocities in order to heal and rebuild their community; where focus on forgiveness hides the need for justice as well. Forgiveness should not replace justice.

Forgiveness should never compromise safety. If you are, or have been, experiencing any anti-love in your life at all – get out of there now and keep your loved ones away from the perpetrator(s) as well. Then report it to the authorities. You can easily forgive the perpetrator(s), if you want to, from a safe distance and it is not your job, and never your responsibility, to fix or heal the perpetrator.

The aim of exercising forgiveness is to ensure that we do not allow the perpetrators to live rent-free in our minds and that we allow ourselves to heal. So if the word, forgiveness, works for you and that you are either happy with the word itself, or you are content with one of the many popular interpretations such as, "Forgiveness means that you let go of the hope that the past could have been different", then you should of course continue to use it. If you, like me, have found that you just cannot make the word work for you then I recommend that you find your own words instead. For example:

Do you want to let go of terror, or fear – in order to feel peaceful, or safe?

Do you want to let go of dirty, or contaminated – in order to feel clean, or pure?

Do you want to let go of not being good enough, or worthless – in order to feel worthy, or loveable?

Do you want to let go of guilt, or shame – in order to feel innocent, or free?

Do you want to forgive, or do you want to release and let go?

Do you want to let go of it (stop holding on to it)? Then let it go (release it)?

After leaving behind the New Age and Christian community pressure to forgive I realized that I cannot actually understand why anybody wants to be forgiven. I do not want to be forgiven. I want to remember what I have done wrong. I want to regret what I have done wrong. I don't have a need for beating myself up about what I have done wrong. I don't have a need to indulge in massive guilt trips over what I have done wrong, but I do want to own it.

For me, forgiveness feels like a power-game and I refuse to take part anymore. When we know that all the perpetrators in this world never chose to become evil, then there is really nothing to forgive, and we can instead just focus all our energy on healing ourselves. I am no longer willing to participate in forgiveness. If somebody wants forgiveness then they will have to forgive themselves.

NLP Timeline experiment:

In my late thirties I tried to see if by changing my story about my upbringing that I could change my current reality. I was inspired by the NLP Timeline technique designed to rewrite your past and therefore putting you in charge of creating your future. It is a technique that takes advantage of our ability to visualize and subsequently feel differently about a past experience that we have had. Having tried the technique during 2 x 10 sessions with two different qualified NLP Therapists, and having short-lived results, I decided to try a different approach. I decided to create a different past for the key family members who were the reason for all the suffering caused to me. I wanted to explore the possibility if I could really, really believe in a better past so that I could then believe in a better present reality. This is how, in short, my revised family story went:

One day at the time when my biological grandmother was carrying my biological mother in her womb, her paedophile husband took the dog for a walk in the rain. He got hit by lightening and died instantaneously. As simple as that. He just died at the hand of Nature; like when the lion hunts down and eats the sick gazelle from the herd. It was nobody's fault. He had to die. [I should mention that I did consider starting at a generation earlier and killing off his psychopath father, who turned his son into a paedophile, but a part of me wanted to make my biological mother's father responsible as he had been influencing my life directly]. The dog, a lovely German Shepherd called Sne, was unscathed and ran home. My biological grandmother cried for a month until she had cried out all her fear and despair. Then her survival instinct for herself and her unborn baby started to kick in, and she began to feel a strong urge for rekindling her joy of swimming. She decided to visit the forest lake in Bøgeskoven (a beech forest belonging to Gjorslev estate not far from the Jurassic coastline called Stevns Klint) and she would swim for almost a whole hour every day. It was because of her love of swimming in this particular forest lake that she met the man who would become my Grandfather.

My Grandfather, Magnus, was a forester and cabinet maker. He loved working with wood. He understood wood. He truly appreciated and respected wood. During winter he would clear up the areas in Bøgeskoven that had been devastated after severe storms. Arriving at the scene, with those 80 feet tall majestic Beech trees scattered around the forest floor, it looked as if a couple of giants had just been disturbed and had left their game of Mikado in a hurry. Magnus would work together with his two draught horses, Frida and Blis, who were the kindest and most gentle 18 hands tall companions anybody could wish for. Frida loved the squeaking sound when walking in snow, and having sunshine on her back; Blis loved the taste of wood sorrels, and getting his feathers wet in the sea. This gentle team would steadily and calmly clear the area. All you could hear was the sound of the chains when Magnus wrapped them around the tree trunks, together with the familiar sounds of the axe and saw. This gentle team knew each other so well that commands such as, "Walk on", and "Back up" were unnecessary, and they would simply tidy up the area with humble respect and honouring Nature to heal and restore the ground in good time.

Bøgeskoven is situated right next to the sea and when you go for a walk, you will therefore get the extra treat of fresh sea air, as well as the sound of the waves and a magnificent sunset over the sea during evening walks. Magnus preferred to start his walks into the beech forest next to the little harbour, then after passing the forest lake on the left, swing right by all the pine trees that then led you out to the sea and those beautiful big beech trees that barely hold on to the shore bank today. It was on one of those walks when he met the woman, Ida, who would become the Grandmother that I wished I had. Magnus was walking past the forest lake one gloriously sunny afternoon when he discovered this woman swimming at an extremely fast pace from one edge of the lake to the other. A big white German Shepherd, with the kindest face, was guarding her from the lake shore. Like an arrow, she would shoot out from the reeds that would then swallow her up on the other side of the lake, and then she would shoot out again - so effortlessly and so elegantly. It was as if special dispensation had been bestowed upon her from the water molecules and that they had agreed to carry her and push her along as was she the Queen Elf of the forest lake. It felt amazingly joyous to witness this relationship between the woman and the water. However this was nothing in comparison to the amazement Magnus felt when he saw Ida getting out of the water - she was heavily pregnant. He felt compelled to walk over and speak to her and express his amazement and admiration. That was the beginning of their life long relationship.

Shortly after their first meeting, Ida and the German Shepherd, Sne, moved in with Magnus in his forest cottage. Magnus was a master craftsman who was often called upon by the famous cabinet maker and furniture designer, Kaare Klint, whenever they received bespoke orders requiring hidden compartments and exquisite inlays. He would craft his furniture in his fully equipped workshop which formed part of the stables that housed Frida and Blis. Magnus took upon the honour of creating the most beautiful baby cot which he finished just in time for the birth of the girl that would become my mother. The cot was made of walnut tree. It was ornamented with exquisite cherry marquetry, rose wood and mother of pearl inlays depicting magical Elves amongst delicate bluebells, cornflowers, roses and mythical creatures. Magnus and Ida loved each other and they loved their daughter who grew up in a loving, caring and safe environment. My mother grew up, wanted and precious, whole and unscathed, and supported in being everything she was and everything she wanted to become.

When I believed this story I felt so relieved and it made me feel so proud of my family. It made me feel so safe. However it only worked momentarily because the horrible true memories would suddenly show their ugly faces, and so I realized that this attempt was not really feasible as it could only ever become yet another short term coping mechanism.

Meditating

I was introduced to meditation in my late teens. In those days I desperately wanted some sort of divine experience from my meditations and all that really happened was that I would eventually fall asleep. For many years subsequently I was only ever able to meditate to guided meditations which, although very useful, were really visualizations rather than meditations. It wasn't really until my early forties when I started to really enjoy meditating. Whereas before, I had meditated because "I really should make an effort to meditate", now I could not wait to get to a clear timeframe during the day where I could enjoy meditating for at least an hour. I found the most comfortable sitting position so that nothing would ache or irritate, and I chose the best music (Healing Earth by Anugama) that would allow me to go on my own journeys whilst supporting me gently along the way. Whenever the weather was dry, I would sit on my patio amongst flowers and a team of buzzing bees and absolutely enjoy meditating. I would usually start by breathing in Love and breathing out Peace and then after a while wait for a word, or on occasion a color, that would take me along on my journey. Sometimes I would know the word immediately and sometimes I would have to go through a series of words or colors, such as freedom, peace, love, light, eternal, thank you, white, purple, blue, green, yellow, orange, red, gold. If I tried to choose a word up front, then I could not get on to my free-flowing journey and the meditation would turn into a forced visualization instead. So I always had to wait for the color or word that would give me access to the space where my journeys take place. When I had entered this space I would have a look around and most often I could see that I had a large white Lotus flower spinning above my head. It was perfect in every sense and it would just hover there a few inches above my head spinning clockwise. I was not able to turn the spinning anti clockwise and I was not able to change the color of the Lotus, I was only able to change the speed of the spinning if I felt it was spinning too fast.

After the Healer, John McGrath, had healed away the big black round stone of evil, as I mentioned earlier, I had two meditations that shifted me: I was meditating amongst the flowers on my patio and I suddenly noticed that a gold ball had appeared in the middle of my Heart Chakra. It was approximately 4 cm in diameter and very soft and malleable. It was very comfortable to carry this gold ball and it felt like an important part of me. Then two days later I had the most beautiful experience: I had entered my space of meditation and when I looked up, I saw that the Lotus spinning above my crown centre was very big and it had turned a vibrant purple. It was so fresh and healthy and strong that it seemed possible to balance an elephant on top of it. It was shimmering and shining and so very beautiful. Then when I looked further up I noticed a sphere. It was about 12 cm in diameter and its thin membrane was made of iridescent plasma. Discovering this sphere filled me with ultimate gratitude and I was in complete awe observing it. After a few minutes it orbited down about one meter in front of me until it was in line with my Heart Chakra and then it moved in very quickly and merged with my Heart Chakra now containing the gold ball. I knew that this sphere was the pure me and it was now safe for it to reside in my body as I was no longer contaminated by the evil I had been carrying. I had finally come home as it was now safe for me to come home. I felt showered by grace and so touched by this. I felt reunited with the pure essence that is me.

5. Facing Belief Head On

I am now an agnostic and so I do not have a problem with other people believing in a God concept. I am however very interested in how we use our God concept as it reveals our level of emotional development and if this is contributing to a loving world or an anti-love ridden world.

From about the age of eleven I carried the possibility of suicide with me as a solution to my suffering. It was my get-out clause for when I was not able to take anymore. And I had as such given myself full permission to end my life when I had run out of survival tricks. I did get very close to exercising my get-out clause on several occasions, and I had 'it all' planned out meticulously. But each time I managed to set in motion my subconscious survival instinct, which would override my decision to 'check out' from this dimension by coming up with some kind of reason for staying alive. Afterwards I would imagine that it was God who had interfered with my plans because God wanted me to stay alive. In my younger days it was often down to method when I couldn't really cope with the thought of how to cut or drown myself combined with the embarrassing mess my body would leave behind. Later on, when I had found the 'perfect method' I managed to conjure up hope loaded possibilities, such as the possibility of getting a new job, finding meaning in creating a new development process, or making connections with people who made it look possible that they could help me get rid of some of my physical symptoms and emotional stumbling blocks. I would imagine that it was God that had created these opportunities so that I could stay alive.

I have thankfully never suffered from depression, which can often cause suicidal thoughts; my suicide option was simply a practical solution to not having to endure all the physical pain and ghastly memories that I was facing on a daily basis. I would often find myself driving home from work with a full-blown migraine, having to stop at every service station on the way to vomit, praying to God that my life could be swapped with somebody else's life. I would repeatedly pray for a cancer known to be deadly within the matter of weeks. And I would pray that my life, without the physical and emotional suffering, got swapped to somebody else who really needed to stay alive – in my view that would be a single mother with a young child; a single mother who truly loved her child and who was capable of bringing up her child in a loving, supporting and safe environment. In between my prayers, I would look out for a 'good' concrete pillar or bridge support along the motorway. I would try to remember approximately where this particular concrete structure was located so that I could drive back late at night when there would be nobody on the roads. Then I could crash into it with precision, at high speed, and without causing harm to anybody else, as well as leaving plenty of time for emergency workers to clean up my mess so that nobody would be late for work the next morning.

I never did get around to driving back to any of the concrete pillars as I would each time have either recovered from the migraine torture a week later, or I would have found a way of pushing the ghastly memories away for a while. God never did give me the cancer I had prayed for either.

The last time I conjured up a reason for staying alive was by realizing that I could not say, with hand on my heart, that I had showed up fully as me in this life. I could not say, with hand on my heart that I had made a real effort to embody the life I had been given. I could not say, with hand on my heart, that I had a right to check out when I had never really checked in fully, and so I decided to stand up, show up, and speak up as me. This coincided with my process of letting go of my hope in God as described in Chapter 1. I had used God as an excuse to stay alive. When I did let go of God it was suddenly up to me to consciously be in charge of my life. It was up to the conscious me if I deemed my life worthy or worthless. It was up to me to decide if I live or die. It was up to me to take full responsibility for my life. And so I made my choice.   I chose my life.   I chose to live my life.   The funny thing is that when you make this kind of choice – there is no going back. I did try and toy with the idea of suicide, at the next violent 3-day migraine attack, and it immediately felt like I had betrayed myself in the highest possible way and so I quickly snapped out of it and never returned. Actually having to choose to live your life has the same power as no longer being able to lie to yourself and this is truly liberating.

When I used to believe in God, I, like so many, used religious scriptures to justify what I felt was right and what I wanted to say or do. For example, to try and prove that we are all capable of creating miracles, heal and do good, I would refer to Jesus' famous quote: "You can do what I did and even greater [paraphrasing]". The fact is that I have absolutely no idea what Jesus said or did. No living soul has any idea what Jesus allegedly said or did. I have of course no way of proving that Jesus even existed, but ancient documents cross referenced with various other ancient letters and documents suggest that a man such as Jesus did exist and so I will go along with that. The oldest Christian scriptures, written by normal unexceptional people – not angels; not God - that exist were created several generations after Jesus and his family passed away. When I realized what I had been doing I wanted to get to the truth of the scripture I had been referring to. I found the scholar, Jeremy Cresswell's book, 'The Invention of Jesus', very helpful as it pointed out that we know that Codex Sinaiticus and Codex Vaticanus were written by unexceptional people who had good days and bad days, who made mistake after mistake whilst copying from other scriptures, and who obeyed orders to alter and tailor passages in order to fit in messages to cater for the emerging Christian Doctrine. Thanks to Bishop Spong I was also reminded of the blatant fact that Jesus was Jewish and the first scriptures were written by Jewish people for Jewish people and then clumsily altered decades later by Matthew who borrowed endless passages from the Old Testament in his attempt to persuade the reader that Jesus was an improved version of Moses. By quoting what Jesus allegedly said I was really no better than those who pick their own quotations from various religions in order to suppress women, homosexuals and other groups of our fellow human beings. Some may argue that my choice of quotation was OK as my intension was to help my fellow human beings. But to somebody else who has been brought up, by their Imam, to believe that the world will fall apart if women are allowed proper education, then they believe that they are doing us all a favor as well by shooting a schoolgirl in the head. And to a grandmother who was brought up to believe that a woman was not worth marrying with her genitals intact believes that she is carrying out the right action when she mutilates the genitals of all the little girls in her community.

The fact is that no matter what religious or cultural doctrine we believe in, we believe in something that other human beings, normal mortal unexceptional human beings from the past, have created. Some of those human beings claimed that they had had some kind of special access to God and that they knew God better than their fellow human beings and that God had a habit of speaking to them. This phenomena is still very much alive and I have, during walking my spiritually conscious path, met people who believe that when they come up with a creative idea or new life purpose that it is something that has been channeled to them via Angels, Ascended Masters and even God, but when they get inspired to action more mundane tasks then it is something they themselves have come up with. I have come across people that were certain that God spoke to them and told them to join a religious community of some sort. I have come across people that were certain they had channeled scriptures of divine importance for all humankind and when you read the content it turned out to be the old common sense à la love your neighbor, but ornamentally written with old fashioned words such as 'thy' and 'thou'. I have come across people who almost died from deadly disease and when recovering following an out of body experience, were certain that they were 'meant to' almost die in order to learn to be less afraid or more present or less judging or more emphatic etc. The thing is that no matter what we experience, conclude and subsequently believe – whether it is based on something we have been told, read or heard, via parents, priests, meditative states, out of body, near death experiences, or general physical, neurological and psychological experiences – we will always be limited by being a human being. No matter how many times we reassure ourselves that we are a soul merely having a human experience and that what we have been experiencing has come about by some divine power, it still, however beautiful it might appear, has to be filtered though our own individual filters and personal agenda of basic conditioning that we have created from the moment we were conceived with subsequent fears, hopes, wishes and needs.

Human beings will some times believe the strangest things – from ancient scriptures to conspirator theories. For example, Channel 4 aired a documentary, 'Big Foot Files', in 2013 where they were visiting countries all over the world where people had reported sightings of Big Foot. A scientist would then take samples of the hair specimens each person had held on to following their encounter with the Big Foot, and the samples would then be checked genetically to establish if it belonged to an already known species or if it was an entirely new species and possibly Big Foot. Each person felt very strongly about the sample they had provided as they were certain that it was indeed Big Foot they had encountered. Some of them had held on to their belief for several decades and had dedicated and centered their entire life around their meeting with the Big Foot. The analysis of the hair samples revealed that they came from various types of bear, dog, deer, cow, and I think there was a raccoon in there as well.

In Ireland they used to believe that the fairy folk could turn up and snatch away young boys at any time of the day and night, and so they would dress their boys in a skirt instead of trousers to fool the fairy folk.

In Denmark the peasants used to believe that a Nisse would live on every farm. A Nisse is a kind of house Hob, Goblin or Brownie. The height varied and some believed he was about 60 cm tall and some the height of a 10 year old boy, but everybody agreed that he was several hundred years old, wore grey clothes and a red woolly hat. Sightings of this Nisse would be very rare and you would now and then hear somebody reporting that they had just by pure luck managed to see a glimpse of his red woolly hat in the staples. The Nisse would be helping the farmer with ensuring a good harvest as well as looking after the animals, for example, if a horse was being particularly healthy then it was because the horse was the favorite of the Nisse. The Nisse would carry out all his good deeds completely voluntarily and all you had to do to keep him happy was to leave a bowl of rice or oat porridge, with a big dollop of butter in the middle, in the staples for him now and then. There were horror stories going around about what could happen if you did not make sure that you kept the Nisse happy. For example, a farmers help had decided to play a trick on the Nisse one day and had left a handful of grit in the porridge. As revenge the Nisse had ensured that the harvest would fail for several consecutive years after this incident.

I have often wondered why we gravitate towards the Messiahs, super-powers and fairytales. What is it that motivates us when we are beaten down by personal misery that we overreach for Nirvana and Super Man instead of just climbing up on the next step in repairing and improving our lives? - even when we know that faith is not the same as truth. Is it because we are so overwhelmed by the misery of our world that we want somebody to just come and take it all away so that we don't have to? Is it because we want somebody to come and save us because we don't believe that we have the power to do it ourselves? Is it because we believe that we are not allowed to be in charge of our lives? I am not sure.

I was using God to avoid taking responsibility for my life. Some people use God to justify their own oppressing and violent actions. Some use God to vent their pent up anger and pain in the shape of carrying out gruesome atrocities. Some use God to reinforce their low self-esteem because of their learned belief that they are worthless sinners. Some use God to attack what they do not understand. Some use God to frighten people into refraining from questioning authority. Some use God to judge themselves and others. Some use God to substantiate their own stance. Some use God to believe that they may get what they wish for from an outside source rather than through personal achievements. Some use God to fall back on when nothing else makes sense. Some use God as an invisible friend. Some use God to feel righteous. Some use God to feel valuable. Some use God to feel accepted. Some use God to feel loved. Some use God as their own conscience and moral compass. Some use God to remind themselves of the good within themselves and other people. Some use God to direct their awe and gratitude for good fortune, nature and all things beautiful in life.

What are you using God for?

6. Are you Following your Heart or your Hope?

My upbringing had taught me that I was completely worthless. As a result I ended up as an adult, attracting relationships with men that were only too happy to prove just that to me. They came in all shapes and sizes, from teachers and businessmen to plumbers and holistic therapists - short, tall, bald, hairy, chubby and skinny – all agreeing that I was unlovable. And so I did put my heart through a few stampedes. The thing is though, that all the warning signs were there from the beginning of meeting each of those men. But I convinced myself that I was 'meant to' meet them in order to learn something about love and fulfilling my soul contract, whilst simultaneously hoping that this man, or the next, would by some miracle learn to love me if only I could learn to become perfect enough. Did I really not think I deserved more and better than that? How could I begin to even consider letting him near me and just hand over my Heart in to his love-forsaken hands each time? - I must have been momentarily insane. And yet, I did. I did because I followed my Hope and not my Heart in spite of hearing great big warning bells and seeing flashing blue lights. In spite of my higher self shouting: "No Noooooooo, not him! He doesn't know how to treat anybody with Love -

including himself". I fell in love with whom I hoped he was, not who he showed me he was.

I followed my hope and not my heart. There is a big, big difference: When you follow your hope you ignore your inner most truth and your most precious essence and you suppress your Love Particle. You go along with something that is not quite right but you hope that something, or someone (that someone can even be God) will make it right along the way. We even go back to anti-love and non-love, only to suffer some more, under the excuse that miracles do happen, and that there are 'unfinished business' that you need to live through or 'find closure' for. Our own defense against our ill-advised decision, or let's say our self-prescribed 'get-out clause' in following our hope is: that although your action will leave you completely empty-hearted, your action will never leave you empty-handed because you will always be able to learn something from all the emotional suffering and for some, physical pain, and come out of the experience with a dose of wisdom. Our core belief then confirms that, that is why you are alive on this planet anyway – our purpose is to learn and do what you are 'meant to be doing'- because that is what God or the Universe has decided you are meant to do. This belief is then supported with the belief that God or the Universe only gives you tasks that you are strong enough to endure. All of this is simply an elaborate coping mechanism – to finding purpose and meaning in suffering in order to endure it.

The human being has developed a sophisticated mental ability to create a host of survival mechanisms. We are capable of calculating risk and action planning when we experience instances that present us with the option to fight, flee or freeze. More interestingly though, we are also able to use our mental gift for story-telling, and so we use our imagination to create meaning out of thin air when life presents us with meaningless violence, natural catastrophe and personal loss. We have as such developed into a species of highly effective self-soothers.

The well known psychiatrist, Victor Frankl, made some great observations of our need for meaning, and he pointed it out clearly when he said: "Man's main concern is not to gain pleasure or to avoid pain but rather to see meaning in his life. That is why man is even ready to suffer, on the condition, to be sure, that his suffering has a meaning". This is why we can send men and women, willingly, into war and cultivate suicide bombers as easy as pie. I used to feel comforted by the belief that it is the Universe, God or Life that forces learning situations, in the shape of suffering, on us - a belief that most Christians, holistic and New Age thinkers hold; now I am completely comfortable believing that suffering is absolutely meaningless as all suffering is created by human beings and can therefore be prevented. I know that we can easily learn all our lessons through Love instead.

Unfortunately, when we believe in giving suffering a purpose and meaning, we develop a very high pain threshold which makes it possible to continuously endure, participate in, endorse and normalize suffering. We then endorse suffering to such a degree that we see meaning in our own and other people's suffering as well. You then hear conclusions like these:

"Oh I see, you were meant to be raped when you were 7 years old so that you could help other child abuse and rape victims later in your life", or, "Oh I see, you were meant to be abandoned by your parents when you were a baby so that you could help other orphans as an adult", or, "Oh I am so sorry that you are going through all of this unbearable pain from losing your child in that school shoot-out, but it is probably because God has a plan for you and your child, and he only gives you challenges that he knows you can endure" or, "Oh I see, your partner was meant to be unfaithful to you so that you could learn to value and love yourself". How about nobody gets raped and nobody gets abandoned in the first place?! How about children are treated as the pure treasures that they are, so that they don't end up as mentally and emotionally crippled people that shoot children in schools and commit terrorist acts all over the world?! How about we are all brought up in Love so that we learn that we are valuable and loveable from birth?! On the account on finding meaning in one's own suffering I have come across this one: "I don't regret having my arms and legs blown off in the war. It has made me a stronger person and I am much more positive now." How about that our Governments invested in renewable energy, including fusion, thus making our countries self sufficient instead of creating wars on the basis of securing oil supplies for the few who profit? And how about the men and women, who thought they would find purpose in fighting their Governments' wars, who are having to find strength they didn't know they had, and who are not able to get through the day without a host of positive thinking techniques after they have returned home with their limbs blown off and their minds blown to pieces – that they were brought up in Love in the first place with the knowing that simply being themselves is all the meaning and purpose they need?

When we give something purpose and meaning, we give it value. When we give something value, we endorse it, we sustain it, we create more of it, we don't do anything to stop or prevent it, and we allow our Governments to prioritize support for war, profit and power for the few - instead of prioritizing the welfare of their people. When you instead see suffering for what it is – anti-love and non-love – you develop a healthy zero tolerance and refuse to endorse, endure and participate in suffering. When you follow your heart you care about what you want and what you need and that is Love – always Love. And the Love we always need is the true kind that actually feels like Love and not like perceived love twisted into the shape of cruel lessons or painful 'Earth Drama'.

When you follow your Heart you choose Love, you repel non-love and put an end to anti-love.

7. Revealing Love

I see no love in sacrifice
and only survival in hope
no honour in death
and never glory from suffering

And now the tricky part - how do we identify what Love really is when non-love and anti-love, the creators of human suffering, have had thousands of years of positive PR, and have either been mistaken for love, or endorsed as necessary and part of God's loving will and plan for us, and a normal and natural component of 'the hand that life deals you'? I think that we have to dig deep - with truth, honesty and compassion for ourselves and for our fellow human beings - so that we can uncover and distil what we have perceived as love and so that we can allow real Love, or even Love Absolute, to emerge - and then turn up the volume on Love. And before we start turning up the volume on Love we need to ensure that we don't inadvertently, and in spite of our good intentions, turn up the volume on what we have already created – non-love and anti-love. So for that we need to do something that is not exactly spiritually correct – we need to judge. I know that this will feel somewhat uncomfortable for hardened New-Agers and all-accepting holistic folk, but we will only be using our judgment in order to acknowledge what love is not. It won't be pretty, and although some of it will be entertaining and even funny, some of it won't be comfortable and so I have created a couple of little breaks in the form of small meditations so that we can hold on to our light along the way. I have written the meditations in first person so that you can slow down and read it to yourself – as opposed to being instructed by me. So, without further ado, and with compassion in hand, let's go forth and commence the distilling process by looking at a series of examples of anti-love and non-love.

Definition of suffering caused by Anti-Love and Non-Love (recap)

Anti-love: Anti-love results in suffering that is created by human beings who cause other people the most terrible, horrific and soul-crushing experiences. Those experiences include: Child abuse and neglect, sexual abuse, Female Genital Mutilation, slavery, sex trade and forced prostitution, emotional and mental abuse, rape, assault, murder, torture, genocide, racism, hate crime, gender oppression, bullying etc.

There is nothing you can learn from anti-love. There are absolutely no lessons and no divine meaning to extract from anti-love. If you are submitted to anti-love then get the hell away from there. Remove yourself from the anti-lover(s) and then report it to the appropriate authorities. If your child is submitted to anti-love, for example bullying, then do not waste a second and **do what ever it takes** to protect your child and find support so that healing can commence immediately.

Non-love: Non-love also results in suffering as it is based on one person's desire for another person to fulfill their need. When you get your need fulfilled – you feel good. There is no element of love being shared or exchanged between two people – it is simply an ego-trip of emotional masturbation run by the non-lover so that they can get a fix of feeling good or avoid feeling bad. To ensure success for the non-lover it is therefore, with the aid of subconsciously driven manipulation, often portrayed as love. A non-lover will most often convince themselves that what they are feeling *is* love because it makes them feel good. So this "love" looks like kind, thoughtful, helpful, generous, protective, passionate, caring and grateful gestures while it slowly sucks the life out of the receiver and steadily corrodes the relationship. Non-lovers are not aware of that their feelings and actions have nothing to do with love.

What non-lovers are deep down really hoping to gain is Love, but they will only ever, at most, gain further non-love in the shape of feeling needed, feeling wanted, feeling important, feeling special or powerful for a short while.

Some people who have been brought up with non-love combined with anti-love have been contaminated so thoroughly that they have become sociopaths or psychopaths – masters of anti-love.

They have become so numb that although they know what they are doing they do not care about that their actions are completely loveless, and the destruction their actions cause. They just resolve to actions that appear to be kind, caring or generous, and that can look like it is founded in love, if they estimate that it is the easiest and quickest way of getting what they want in a given situation.

Both anti-love and non-love can create victims as well as survivors; it can create more non-lovers, and it can create more anti-lovers.

A declaration of love, "I love you", coming from a non-lover or an anti-lover is completely worthless to the receiver and even has the power to cause tremendous harm.

Incompetent parents are often very good at running non-love ego-trips on their children. This is why generation after generation has grown up believing that fulfilling other people's needs shows that we love them, and that it will result in us being loved back. We have grown up to believe that somebody loves us very much when they declare they will do anything for us. The compounded harm and suffering resulting from non-love inflicted on children is that they may grow up to become 'people pleasing' adults who go through a whole life without ever managing to experience Love.

A common parental non-love example is when parents expect 'payment in kind' for bringing their child into this world. I have met a mother who got pregnant for the sole reason that she expected that she would be loved by her child. I have met mothers who felt an inherent ownership and right to have access to their children's children, and would refer to them as '**My** grand children'. I have met mothers and fathers who decided to have a child because they hoped it would save their marriage. I have met mothers and fathers who expect their children will look after them in their old age. I have met mothers and fathers who do everything they can to coerce their children into becoming what they themselves failed to be. I have met mothers and fathers who saw nothing wrong in using their children to avoid feeling lonely after a break-up. This kind of non-love is of course not consciously malicious – it is just a series of incidents of parents trying to get their needs met from the wrong source.

Another non-love example relating to perceived parents' love is when they sacrifice themselves for their children. You hear people say: "She sacrificed herself for her children by always putting them first and she last. And she drove them to football and dance lessons and even took an extra job to pay for it all – that is a mother's love for you". I am sorry but there is no love in parental sacrifice. There is however plenty of guilt trips, fear and always, always, always choice in sacrifice. Parental sacrifice is usually based on over-compensating for their own childhood which has left them with a feeling of perpetual lack; lack of love, lack of safety and other basic needs not being fulfilled. There is a choice based on the perception that an action is worth suffering for; that the other person, or cause, is worth more than the person offering the sacrifice. If an action feels like sacrifice, especially in respect of parenting, then somebody made a choice founded in suffering – not Love.

For many, many years we have promoted the 'sacrifice equals love case'. I suspect that it stems from the Christian community who will often refer to the story that Jesus sacrificed himself on the cross for his love of human kind; even that God sacrificed his own son through this act. In our eagerness to promote sacrifice we have tried to stick it on emergency workers such as fire fighters and similar people in high-purpose jobs - as they put themselves through terrifying, life threatening or truly exhausting ordeals in order to save other people's lives. And so pure sacrifice, and therefore altruism, is often attributed to their actions. Emergency workers have my utmost gratitude, respect and admiration. Not only do they save people's lives, but because they save people's lives they prevent numerous hearts from being crushed and lives from being shattered on a daily basis. Part of my respect is also grounded in the knowledge that they have undergone extensive training in calculating risk, within seconds, in order to stay safe whilst pulling people out of burning buildings. If they stay safe then they can save more people as well. If sacrifice was their purpose for going to work, then we would have to assume they were all mentally ill akin to Kamikaze pilots and suicide bombers alike. And I rest assured in the knowledge, that they would willingly pull an overweight chain-smoking middle-aged man out from the roaring flames, but refuse, point blank, if we asked them to donate their own heart in order to save that same man via a heart transplant the next day.

You will often come across non-love relationships where both spouses are running their individual ego-trips. They often succeed in keeping the relationship going for many years - even to death do them part - by skillfully buying and selling their respective needs. For example (stereotypically): She got married to him because she wanted children. He got married to her because he did not want to die alone. She wanted to feel worthy by finally being with a man that did not let her down. He wanted to feel needed by being the hero that finally didn't let her down. He wants to feel like a good husband by buying her tulips (his mother's favorite flower) every Friday. She hates tulips but always says thank you, smiles and put them in a vase, and places them on the kitchen windowsill because she does not want to appear ungrateful. She wants to feel like a proper wife by always using starch on his work shirt collars. He hates the feeling of the stiff collar on his neck every morning but thanks her for ironing his shirts because he does not want to appear ungrateful. She cooks his favorite meal every Saturday. He decorates the house in her desired color scheme once a year. She gets to criticize him on a daily basis; this gives him permission to flirt with Mandy from marketing on second floor. When she feels angry she likes to blame him for when he wasn't present at the birth of their first born son. He counter attacks, feeling righteous, as he clarifies that he wasn't there because he had to meet an important customer, thus securing a large bonus, so that he could pay for her staying at home with their first born son. She feels safe having a husband. He feels like a proper man, having a wife. She feels wanted when they are having considerate sex (considerate sex as opposed to making love). He feels loved when they are having considerate sex. She buys expensive designer handbags; this gives him permission to pay for his expensive country club golf membership. She wants him to share her passion for attending yoga retreats. He doesn't like yoga but goes along because he likes the attention from all the other women. He wants her to attend the company Christmas party with him. She thinks his colleagues are boring but goes along because she likes dressing up and being admired by his colleagues. Being married to him prevents her from feeling lonely. Being married to her prevents him from feeling lonely.

Non-Love is thriving in relationships when people say, "I love you", and their love declarations are based on having a specific need met so that they can feel good or avoid feeling bad:

"I am saying that I love you (because you always say you love me, and I do not want to hurt you by not reciprocating)"

"I am saying that I love you (because I want you to be 'The One' for me and I am hoping that the wonderful story I have made up about you can become true)"

"I am saying that I love you (because I feel that my life has purpose and is meaningful with you as my partner)"

"I am saying that I love you (because the way you are treating me makes me feel special, or wanted, or worthy, or safe, or……insert your own word……)"

"I am saying that I love you (because it makes me feel wanted when we are having sex)"

"I am saying that I love you (because I care about you)"

"I am saying that I love you (because you are willing to do all the things my previous partners did not want to do)"

"I am saying that I love you (because I no longer feel lonely when you are in my life)"

"I am saying that I love you (because you treat me better than my previous partners)"

"I am saying that I love you (because I feel that I own you, and that makes me feel powerful)"

"I am saying that I love you (because I feel responsible for you, and that makes me feel important)"

"I am saying that I love you (because you tell me that you need me, and that makes me feel wanted)"

"I am saying that I love you (because I feel that I need you)"

"I am saying that I love you (because I do not believe that I am capable of carrying on without you)"

"I am saying that I love you (because you are helping me)"

"I am saying that I love you (because I believe that you can save me, or heal me, or cure me, or protect me, or……insert your own word…….)"

"I am saying that I love you (because I want you to love me)"

"I am saying that I love you, and you and you and you as well, (because I want people to believe that I am a nice person)"

"I am saying that I love you (because I feel good when you are in my life)"

I have certainly been guilty of the top three statements. In respect of the first declaration: I had a friend who said that she loved me. I did not love her. I did not need or want her to love me. I cared about her. So I never said: "I love you too". Instead I left out the 'I' and reciprocated with, "Love you", or, "Love you too". I did not clarify to her that I did not love her in the way she described she loved me because I did not want to hurt her. We usually do not want to hurt people by telling them our truth because we are afraid that they will then not like us, or that it will result in some kind of loss or negative consequence. I was afraid of telling her my truth as I hoped we could develop a good friendship.

In respect of the second declaration: I had met a man who said that he had been told by four psychics that he would meet somebody exactly like me, and that he had fallen in love with me *a little bit*. I translated that into the presumption that he wanted me to be 'the one' for him [I know, I might as well write 'IDIOT' across my forehead]. I felt that I had known him for a thousand years, and I managed to convince myself that, that feeling was simply love. I so wanted to believe that we were 'meant to be' together. I so wanted him to be the one for me even though I could not feel his heart at all; even though I felt nothing when he kissed me; even though he treated me like a mistress (like shit); even though he had disclosed that he had gone from having sex every day to having had none for several weeks (and this was a very long time for him), which should have alerted me to the possibility that he was perhaps not so much guided by his psychics and ascended masters, as he was by the nether region of his torso. But I made up a wonderful story about him being able to fulfill my needs: that as he was a holistic therapist he would have worked with himself extensively, and would be conscious about his every emotion and subsequent action; that he would not instigate a relationship purely on basic instinct and initial attraction; that he was able to really hear me and see me and sense me – and therefore love the real me, that he would be supportive of me in my work and that we would be a real trail-blazing peace team together. So I declared my "love" for him (a totally worthless love declaration) because I so wanted him to be the one that I could share true love with, and I hoped that this could become reality in time. And so I 'followed my hope' by believing the story I had created about him and us for a few months - until I woke up to smell the non-love.

In respect of the third love declaration, I am guilty of this one as well: Upon meeting each of my partners I have found myself putting aside my work and stepping off my path, and instead making my life all about my partner which I imagined was a true gentleman that was capable of loving me. I did this because I felt that it was much easier to believe that the relationship was my real life purpose. This belief was grounded in my hope that there was a chance that I could get my needs met. In those days that would have been to feel safe, to feel protected, to feel valued - and to feel loved. It felt much easier if a man would come along and love me so that I didn't have to.

It can be very confusing when somebody tells you that they love you but at the same time use you or treat you like somebody they have very little or no care for. Those people are again running their individual ego-trips and can belong in both the anti-love and the non-love categories. Those people manage to generate a feeling, presumably aided by the bonding hormones Oxytocin, Prolactin, and maybe even Vasopressin, that they interpret as love when they think of the story and assumptions they have made up about you, and when they spend time with you.

In the anti-love category a typical example is when grossly incompetent parents "love" their children: If you ask parents that abuse and neglect their children if they love their children, they will confirm that this is very much the case. They will usually also insist that they would never do anything to hurt their children. They use their destructive connection with the child to generate 'that loving feeling' for themselves whilst at the same time annihilating their child in the process. They are convinced that they love their children. My biological mother was convinced that she loved my sister and me. Anti-love parents will often tell their children that they love them - in spite of all the "wrong doing" that they decide the child has accomplished. This is one of the reasons we have created generation after generation for many centuries who believe that parents who beat their children do it **because** they love their children – hence the classic statements: "This is for your own good", and, "It hurts me more than I am hurting you".

Some paedophiles believe that they love the children that they abuse. They believe that their own sexual orientation is that they are simply attracted to children instead of adult women and men, and that they are therefore not abusing the children but instead making love with them. Other paedophiles are of course fully aware that they are molesting the child. Other sexual abusers, irrespective of their age or sex, often convince themselves that because they are successful in making their victim participate in their evil act, that the abuse is something they are 'doing together'.

Another typical anti-love example is the abusive relationships where one spouse is abusing their 'beloved' violently whether it be physically or mentally and emotionally. They will often, to immense harm, declare their "love" after each attack which confuses their victim to such as degree that they stay in the relationship even though their lives, and often their children's lives, are in grave danger. Sadly, we end up in these relationships in the first place because we were brought up to believe we are worthless and un-loveable.

In the non-love category you will find friendships that are affected but that has gone undetected: I had a friend who had convinced herself that she loved me as one loves a close friend. We had met through our mutual New Age interests. And even though she was motivated by escaping in it - and had created a typical 'fairy loving earth angel' persona to go along with it - and I was motivated by developing through it, we both wanted to make the world a better place, and we should as such have been able to create a positive friendship. She told me that she loved me so, so much and that I was so, so important to her as I was her closest friend. And yet, she was quite happy to keep me waiting for half and whole hours+ in cafés and at home when we had arranged to meet. When she finally showed up she would serve me some fabricated BS story as to why she was late and apologize profusely, and then she would do it all again the next time. She would not stick to dates and times we had agreed to speak on the phone, and there she would also serve me one of her fabricated BS stories as to why she had not kept her side of the agreement. She would lie about everything: from the tiniest insignificant things, such as her personal preference of whether it be this plate with the red rim versus that plate with the blue rim - to simply not answering with the truth when I asked her a direct question. This would also be expressed in her need to manipulate instead of asking honestly and directly when she wanted something from me and people around her, or if she wanted to avoid being caught in treating her friends disrespectfully. This was often done in a "psychic revelation" performance, for example: "I *felt* to ask you if you would attend my open day for the new cosmetics pyramid scheme that I have joined?", or, "*I feel that the angels would like me to* charge a fee for inviting people around for a gathering", or if she had blown yet another agreement to speak on the phone, "Oh, then we were probably *not meant to* speak". She would twist my good intensions into personal attacks: for example, concerned for her health (as she was suffering with ME), I warned her against cooking food in her aluminium saucepan, as it could leak heavy metals into her food (which she as an ME sufferer could be extra sensitive to), and I suggested that she only use her saucepans made of stainless steel for cooking. She translated that into that I thought, and had told her, that her saucepans were cheap and of very poor quality. She would repeat my opinions and aha-moments, that I had reached and shared with her, often word for word a couple of weeks later as if they were her own. She would wipe off her childhood victim projections on me like one would wipe dog poop off one's shoe, and she would call me controlling when I didn't feel like doing what she wanted to do.

Now, she could not help it as she had obviously had a tough beginning to her life. This had taught her to lie and manipulate in order to keep safe and to get what she needed for her survival. And as she found that a lot of people still responded favorably to her survival tricks in her adult life, she did not see a need to change. One of her survival tricks was to generate feel-good fixes for herself. To be able to create these feel-good fixes she would give presents (bought on credit cards that she could not afford) or carry out gestures that she expected would result in a positive response such as: "thank you, you are so thoughtful", "thank you, I love you too", "thank you, what a nice surprise". The problem with this was that I did not want to receive any of this – especially as it always came a week after I had called her at our agreed time and left a message. I just wanted a friend I could count on. Even though I told her I did not want it, she carried on anyway. This then resulted in the even bigger problem: that I did not want to be used as her means of feeling good by having to act grateful for something I did not want. And as she did not listen, I coped by simply throwing out her presents and ignoring her gestures. I feel that a present or a kind gesture is only a present and a kind gesture if it is given to give - not to get, and if the receiver actually wants that present or gesture. The only time when 'giving to get' is useful, is when people donate their time or money to good causes such as charities. The donation makes the giver feel good and guilt-free (this is what they 'get'), and the money or time will benefit the good work of the charity. There are of course also people that donate to charities simply because it is an important cause to support as an urgent issue needs fixing, that it is simply the right thing to do.

Towards the end of our "friendship" I coped with my friend's desire to be late and her accompanying BS fabrications by finding practical ways of meeting up with her without having to waste my time waiting for her as well as being spared from yet another insulting BS story. So I would never invite her home to my place unless I was inviting somebody else as well: then this other person could pick her up on the way, or if traveling separately, this other person would arrive on time and we could begin without her. I would also not arrange to meet at an outside venue unless I would pick her up on the way. Most times I would insist on meeting at her place, as I expected her to at least be at home. I did consider using another technique used by fellow sufferers who have "friends" that need to be extremely late – where they tell the "friend" a start time one hour earlier than needed, but I did not want to participate in this type of lying game. This elaborate action plan extended our 'friendship' by a couple of years. After 17 years of trying to navigate this non-love friendship by always conceding that she could not help it as she had had a tough childhood (tougher than mine), combined with my belief that I should be able to transform negative experiences within myself, I reached the point in my life where my self worth had increased to a level where I could honestly say: "My life is precious", and so it became more and more uncomfortable to spend my time and energy in this friendship. To be more exact, it became absolutely intolerable. I could not rely on her or count on her. I did not believe a word she said which made me realize that I did not know who she actually was. She did not know who I was either as she would twist what I said into weird and often negative interpretations – the true words I said was not the words she chose to hear. One of the reasons for this peculiar 'truth lost in translation' phenomenon was that she found it extremely hard to cope with direct and honest talk as she had always, out of fear of rejection and negative reactions, wrapped up her own words in manipulation and pretend fairy glitter, and so she needed other people to do the same. I expect honest and direct communication in a close friendship. Without honesty - emotional intimacy is impossible.

I also realized that I had wasted several days of my life purely on waiting for her in the time I had known her - and that was life spent very, very, very badly indeed.

When I tried to save our friendship, by writing to her; testing if we could build a new friendship based on truth and consideration, and hoping that she would reveal her real self, it transpired that the level of non-love was much, much worse than I had first anticipated and the whole exercise became rather ugly indeed. I found it extremely disturbing to discover how she came up with further lies, instead of surrendering to the truth; how she interpreted my actions, and how she twisted my reactions to her treatment of me. And so I had to concede that we were a million miles apart – and that we always had been. This was particularly hard to swallow. In all the time I had known her I had listened to her interpreting the words and actions of her other friends, and boyfriends, in her peculiar twisted way, and I naively thought, or rather wanted to believe, that because she loved me so, so much as her closest friend, that she did not treat me in the same way. She used to say that she loved me *as I am*, and I suddenly realized that she had "loved" me *in spite* of all the negative things she had made up about me. It was certainly not me that she had loved. She wanted me to love her *as she was* and with that she meant all her lying, manipulating and inconsiderate behavior and just dismiss it as her charming and quirky idiosyncratic personality. I felt absolutely horrified to discover the level of nasty stories she had made up about me, and I felt so sad and so disappointed that the beautiful 17 year friendship story that I had believed turned out to be an illusion. We had both suffered in this non-love friendship: me because of how she treated me, and she because of how she interpreted what I said to her. So I wished her love and ended this non-love friendship. It was truly liberating. It took away a huge load of stress from my every day life and I suddenly felt that I could breathe again.

I am sharing this lengthy story with you, without covering up the blunt edges of the reality of it, and probably causing a few jolts in the guilt over judgment departments, because: friendships (especially friendships in the spiritual development and religious communities where you are taught 'to turn the other cheek' or be all-accepting) often disappear under the radar, when we look at our self-worth and the direct correlation between our self-worth and the caliber of relationships we participate in. We are fully aware that low self-worth attracts unhealthy romantic relationships and we are quite used to hearing recounts about toxic husbands, wives, girl-and boyfriends. But perhaps because it is our friendships that we go to, to recover after each heart break that we endure, and to 'unload' when our boss has had one of their fits again, and to share our most intimate life experiences, we tend to endure non-love in friendships for much longer than we would a romantic non-love relationship. Friends are the family we chose ourselves; they often replace biological family members as well, and so perhaps we find it difficult to let go of unhealthy friendships because they are our only 'safe house' position we can always fall back on.

The fact is though that any relationship, whether romantic, friend or work relation, all serve as an indicator of the level of our self-worth. If any of those relationships are negative in any way at all, then we still have some healing to do.

Oh, the stories we make up about each other

Through self-enquiry we quickly discover the stories we make up about ourselves. And we become experts in recognizing when we are either beating ourselves up or twisting the truth in our favor. Throughout my lifetime, I have also through self enquiry discovered the stories I have made up about other people; often attributing wonderful and positive traits – like the 'four psychics boyfriend' that I mentioned earlier. Now and then, and often by chance, I have also learned to my great shock and amazement, the peculiar stories people have made up about me - like as earlier mentioned, my family who interpreted my withdrawn and pensive teenage demeanor as that I was being cold and cynical. Here are a few others from the particularly disturbing selection, illustrating that people will happily wipe their childhood victim projections off on you, as well as utilizing you for their emotional masturbation fabrications. It also proves my point that my low self-worth has attracted some pretty unsavory people in my adult life:

The Nine West Dominatrix: I was working at a company that needed photographs taken of the premises for some promotional brochures. The freelance photographer who came to take the pictures managed to weave into our small talk conversation that he believed that I was into S&M because of the heels of the boots I was wearing; they had a very thin heel - almost as if the shoemaker had hammered in a nail and coated it with leather. You think I am into what???!!!! The truth about how I came to wear those very boots is this: I needed a new pair of black ankle boots as my trusted old pair was worn out. I ploughed through every shop in my town and neighboring town as well, and ended up in a department store as my last resort. There was this Nine West pair which had a round toe, which I liked, but unfortunately had this really inharmonious and down-right ugly heel that I did not like in any way. I tried them on and they were surprisingly comfortable and easy to walk in and they were not too high either. I stood looking at them for almost 30 minutes, trying to work through that I had not been able to find my perfect pair of ankle boots, could no longer wear my old pair, couldn't think of another shop to try, was tired and bored with the whole issue, did not like the ugly heels, but really liked the round toe. I conceded that whilst wearing them, I would only be able to see the round toe, which I liked, and not be able to see the ugly heel which I did not like at all, and as they were so comfortable, I decided to buy the ankle boots. For crying out loud!!!!

The vile and creepy A-lister: I had helped the door-man of a 5-star hotel in Copenhagen with getting rid of the arthritis in his hand, and he then got me a freelance job as a masseuse at the hotel. The hotel was often frequented by top level business folk as well as politicians and movie stars. A very famous American male movie star was staying at the hotel as he was promoting his film in Copenhagen and he had asked for a massage. When I turned up he was acting kind a humble and I thought to myself how nice he was. He said he was suffering with leg cramps, because he had broken a toe whilst he was in Germany, and so he wanted me to only massage the back of his legs whilst he was lying face down. As it turned out he was actually using the movements of the massage to masturbate until he ejaculated as he thought it was perfectly acceptable to pretend I was a prostitute. I was completely shocked and confused and tried to tell myself that he couldn't help it and that it had been an unfortunate accident and that he was probably very embarrassed, and so I pretended that nothing had happened. I even proceeded to show him some leg stretch exercises afterwards which revealed that I had not shaved my lower legs recently and that made me feel extremely embarrassed. I should instead have shouted: "What in the hell are you doing you filthy piece of shit! You vile disgusting creep! How fucking dare you disrespecting me like this!!!!!", and then call the police.

The Disapproving Silent Treatment Girlfriend: I had a boyfriend who liked to go fishing in weekends. He would leave very early on a Saturday morning and come home in the afternoon on a Sunday. As I have mentioned earlier, I have suffered a lot from violent migraines over the years, and sometimes I would be under attack in weekends when he went fishing. I would send an SMS to him to let him know that I had a migraine so that he knew that I was very ill and not my usual cheerful self. When he came home I would often just have managed to crawl out of bed, still feeling worse for wear, contemplating learning to eat and drink again, and with my brain still not working properly - trying to make sense of the world in a quiet sloth like pace. Through a mutual friend, I learned that he had interpreted my behavior as 'giving him the silent treatment' because he had imagined that I disapproved of him going fishing. This was in spite of me showing interest in, and supporting his angling interests in general, buying him an expensive bait boat (yes there is such a thing in the angling world) for Christmas, and never uttering a negative word about fish and all things angling.   For goodness sake!

The Insemination Proposal: I went to my local health food store one day to pick up a few things. A man saw me and proceeded to strike up a conversation. He told me he was a retired lawyer, had just sold his apartment in London, was into spiritual development and single. He asked me if I was single, to which I confirmed but suggested that a friend of mine might just be something for him if he was looking for a partner. My friend was closer to his age and would find it important that he was a lawyer and had a bit of money as well as being into spiritual development. We exchanged business cards and he suggested we meet up. I subsequently emailed him, informing him that I had told my friend about him and that she would be interested in meeting him. He suggested I visited him where he lived. Not having attempted any kind of matchmaking before, I thought this was a good idea so that I could get a better idea of who he was, and hopefully confirm that I was not trying to send my friend into the arms of a potential axe-murderer. When we met up we exchanged further personal facts and I shared with him that I would turn 40 a few months later. He asked me if I had any children, to which I replied that I had decided long ago that I was not at all interested in having children at any time ever, but that my friend did have a grown up son, and this gave rise to me establishing that he didn't have children of his own. Later on in conversation he managed to inform me, with a 'nudge, nudge, wink, wink' glint in his eye, that he saw himself fathering a child for a 36 year old woman. I found this information not exactly compatible with him meeting up with my friend and wondered what the 'nudge nudge wink wink' was all about and where he had got this idea from – perhaps via a clairvoyant session? Following this harmless but slightly peculiar meeting I told my friend that I wasn't exactly sure that he would be boyfriend material, but that he could perhaps attend a meditation group day in the future so that she could make up her own mind. A couple of months later I met him at my local grocery shop where I was buying food for my 40th birthday celebration that I was hosting the same evening. He asked me how I was and I said I was in a particularly good mood as it was my 40th birthday.   He was astonished as he thought I was 36.   I despair!!!!! He must have turned momentarily deaf at the exact time when I had been talking.

The Nasty Friend Punisher: The 'fairy loving earth angel ex-friend' I mentioned earlier shared with me (in the form of a written accusation) what had gone on in her head towards the end of our non-love friendship when she had yet again turned up extremely late for dinner at my house: She accused me of not wanting to speak to her properly or hug her because I wanted to punish her by withdrawing my love for her, and only when I felt that she had hurt enough and had learnt her lesson would I decide to forgive her and either decide to talk to her or give her a hug. She added that she had now realized how wrong she was to have accepted my treatment of her – showing I was cross by withdrawing my love from her.   I am sorry - you think I am withdrawing what, because I want to do what, until you have done what? – Are you flaming kidding me???!!!   First she treats me like poop and then she manages to make herself the victim. So I had to explain to her that the actual truth was that when I am treated like poop by people that are supposed to be my friends then I hurt. And after many years of being in the receiving end of her need to be extremely late I was being less and less able to cope. I was hurting because she was treating me like that again and again and again and again, but especially because she thought it was ok to serve me some BS lie as to why she was late again when she in reality had just not left home in good time. Because I was hurting and was increasingly not able to cope with her overall treatment of me, I really wanted her to just leave and go home again but I was afraid of saying that as that would hurt her [and I was still, at the time, holding on to the belief that she could eventually be a good friend]. So at the moment when she finally turned up, my happy anticipation of looking forward to seeing my friend had changed to hurt, and I was struggling with pulling myself together by desperately trying to think about something to say to get the conversation going until I had recovered from the worst of the usual let down. I find it repulsive to hug people that treat me like poop and so I usually have to wait until I have recovered enough. So it is all about coping with the pain, finding ways of improving the situation as quickly as possible and then ending up carrying on as normal. I was absolutely amazed to find out that she expected people to just take any crap from her without allowing us some sort of reaction. And it was so very saddening, and really rather creepy, to discover that she then chose to attribute my reaction to some sort of nasty power game that she had dug up from her selection of childhood victim projections. Eeeeuuuw! Get it off me!!!

The Scandinavian Porn Star Delusion: Quite a few of my ex-boyfriends has, upon meeting me, generated great expectations of me being able to fulfill their Scandinavian porn star fantasy. As I had not in any way indicated that porn was one of my many interests, and that I never wear 'sexy' or revealing clothes, I suspect that their expectations were grounded in the fact that I am Danish, and that Denmark was one of the first countries to produce explicit pornographic movies in the 60'ies, which has resulted in peculiar rumors that 'Danish girls are like this or like that, and willing to do all sorts of vile weirdo stunts in the sack'. One of my ex-boyfriends had a substantial collection of porn movies, and he was even expecting that he and I could watch them together. What?! No! Get the hell out of my life!!!! In those days my self-worth was extremely low, and I therefore tried to be understanding by referring to Allan and Barbara Pease's book, 'why men lie and women cry', which describes that men's keen interest in pornography is because they are simply 'visual beings' and that what they are in reality doing is looking at shapes and curves and [subconsciously] considering if the porn star can carry his genes [yes, you may laugh here]. When my self-worth improved, I honored my truth instead: As it happens, I vehemently detest pornography in all its entirety. I absolutely loathe all the prostitution that it tries to whitewash under the excuses of 'supply & demand' and 'free will' (no human being brought up in love would freely choose a life in porn and prostitution). I find it utterly appalling that any human being finds it acceptable to support and keep this soul destroying business sector alive. I also find it alarming that younger generations, with their easy access and exposure to porn, via smart phones etc., have developed completely twisted expectations about how a naked woman or man actually looks like naturally. They are learning from porn that men and women should have implants and various other types of cosmetic surgery, be of a 'certain size', shape and weight, and that love making is shared as a porn performance. Research now shows that even pre-teens believe that they will somehow have to live up to various aspects of the porn image – even hard core. "Voluntary" pornography is non-love at its ugliest, and I am deeply saddened that so much human life is wasted in this way.

I think we can safely assume that we have all been guilty of making up stories and assumptions about other people. And we can also safely assume that other people have made up stories about us – some positive, some negative and some down right creepy. We cannot help it though as we are constantly bombarded with our own reference system that we have meticulously built up from the moment we are conceived and that we continue to add to throughout our lives. We have thousands of reference points that we can use for any situation we come across so that we can attribute meaning to no matter what we experience. This works well for instances like when we hear a baby cry and we assume that this means that the baby needs our assistance because it is either hungry, tired, in pain, is afraid or needs a clean nappy. It does not work so well for instances when we see a woman cry and we assume that she is crying because she wants to manipulate us to take some sort of action in her favor (because this is how our own mother used to behave in order to get our father to succumb to her needs). It could be that this woman is crying because she is afraid, or sad, or angry or even relieved or happy, and so it would be more useful to establishing the truth instead of drawing direct conclusions based on our reference system from our childhood projections department.

Which personal suffering in your life are you giving meaning, extracting purpose from or normalizing?

Where in your life are you participating in (causing or enduring) non-love?

What anti-love are you endorsing (deeming as normal, unavoidable or necessary) in your local environment and in our world?

What can you stop participating in right now?

What can you stop endorsing right now?

Meditation Break

I don't know about you, but I need a little break from all the anti-love and non-love, so I would like to invite you to slow down (and slow down the speed in which you are reading) and join me on one of my personal meditation journeys that I use when I want to let go of my thoughts about people or issues:

I sit at the very end of a calm river in India. The water is so pure that you can see every detail of the river bed. The gentle early evening chorus of the surrounding forest has started to replace the bustle of the bright sweltering day. The light is slowly turning from golden to indigo blue. You can hear the sound of the Tambura playing as one continuous Ohm. The river banks are supported by beautiful red sand stone masonry work depicting Hindu deities, trees, flowers and mythical creatures. I sit comfortably amongst purple, gold, orange, turquoise and magenta silk and velvet pillows. I watch every person I have been thinking about being helped gently into little wooden boats by their personal assistants. If I have been thinking about a person that I find particularly toxic, then they will be picked up in a super fast power boat, or a team of Special Forces will zip wire down from a helicopter, airlifting the toxic person, and taken away immediately to an event that they will enjoy. If I have been thinking about an issue, I see a word or a symbol of the issue being placed in a basket and carried on board by an assistant. The wooden boats are furnished with a comfortable velvet seat and silk pillows in vibrant colors, and they are powered by a white sail that catches the gentle breeze. The lantern at the bow of each boat lights up the face of its passenger and you can see that they look content and exited about their journey. I watch the boats floating down the river away from me. And as the boats float away, the water behind them fills up with Lotus flowers – the Lotus flowers can be any color I want, maybe blue, purple, pink, yellow, orange or white. I see that each boat becomes smaller and smaller and smaller and smaller until they have disappeared from the horizon - and the river is now filled with Lotus flowers. I gaze upon this pure beauty for as long as I want, and then I close my eyes with the knowledge that I am Free. I am completely Free – now and always. I listen to the Tambura guiding me to complete peace. When I open my eyes again I see in front of me an exquisite Lotus flower only lit up by the light of a little oil lamp. I pick it up gently with both hands and then I place it in my Heart Chakra. When I am ready, I stand up - ready to go forth with the Lotus in my heart, and then I return to this other world.

If India, velvet, silk and Lotus flowers is not your thing then you can easily create another scene – cargo ships leaving the Port of Shanghai, trucks and limousines driving away from your street, canoes being paddled away from your tropical island, hot air-balloons lifting up around you – whatever works and creates a liberating and peaceful feeling.

8. The Act of Loving

Choose love over fear
Choose love over loyalty
Choose love over sense
Choose love over survival
Choose love over knowledge
Choose love over complacency
Choose love over belief
Choose love

Being alive in this world is all about relationships. And the relationships of today's world are saturated by a whole lot of non-love.

When we start living from Love, or even Love Absolute, our motivation shifts from buying and selling our needs to living in truth. Our motivation will change from 'covering our arse' to simply 'living truth'. We are then taking action – not to ensure that they are nice to you, not to keep him calm, or to prevent her from getting angry, or to keep her from leaving, or to stop him from hating, or to make her happy, or to keep him keen, or to make her smile, or to stop him from disapproving, or to stop her from losing interest, or to keep the relationship interesting, or because we need to - but because we want to. When we are living Love - our actions show our truth.

Love cannot thrive where truth is absent. Love cannot be applied, or shared, or exchanged without truth.

You cannot love another person unless you are willing to, and succeed in, really seeing, hearing and sensing that person. You cannot be loved unless you are willing to show up in the relationship **exactly** as who you are. A love declaration is worthless to you if you are not truly seen, heard and sensed for all that you are. This of course can be somewhat tricky as a lot of us quickly drew the conclusion, at a very young age, that being exactly who we were was not safe and would result in negative consequences. And so we took upon ourselves to become what we imagined other people wanted us to be instead. And because it resulted in a safer and more comfortable life, and even rewarded us with people liking us, we thought that not being ourselves would reward us with love. That is why we often try to be something we imagine, based on little hints or scrambled information, that the object of our attraction will want. But alas, the truth is that nobody - not your parents, not your beloved and not your friend - will be able to love **you** if you pretend to be somebody and something else instead of being **you** all of the time. They will simply end up loving the lie of you - that 'somebody and something else' that you are pretending to be – instead of loving **you** – the **True**

You. And so you must leave behind your alter ego, your super hero self, your altruistic self, your hard-nosed and hairy-arsed self, your people pleasing self and your belittling self, and then show up in the relationship exactly as who you are because love cannot be exchanged or shared where truth is absent, and a truly loving relationship will therefore otherwise be impossible.

For the seasoned self-developer it is easy to feel love and be love whenever we put our heart and mind to it. However, in order to be able to truly honour our human experience we need to live love as well. We cannot rest on our pretty altruistic laurels and just satisfy ourselves with the notion that all human beings are merely love when we interact with each other; we need to get stuck in and really see, and hear, and sense that person. It can be helpful to understand differences and qualities in the beginning by applying Enneagrams, star signs and other systems that identify human traits to ease communication, but then we need to venture beyond into unknown territory. We need to enquire and listen with all our heart and resisting any assumptions and analysis throughout. We need to meet our fellow human being as equal and lovable whilst resisting any assumptions, pre-determined stories and perceived abilities or disabilities whether positive or negative.

In order to truly love another person romantically we must be able to show up completely as who we really are. And we must succeed in knowing our beloved without fabricating any stories, attributes and potential about them. For that we must know ourselves enough to detect when we are making up stories, based on our needs, hopes and fears about ourselves and our beloved.

Most often we fall in love with the **potential** of the object of our desire following initial biologically chemical input (how they look, sound and smell), and spiritual input (how they feel like), as we reach for our subconscious conditioned emotional references by fabricating a wish list of attributes that would suit our respective needs (it is during this phase that we are particularly good at convincing our self that we are only following our heart): I think he will be a good father to my future children. I think my mother will like her. I think he will be emotionally strong enough to attend our family gatherings. I think she won't mind wearing a Bat Girl costume for me. I think he won't mind fixing my garden shed. I think she will enjoy the local swingers' parties with me. I think he will be able to accept my 'free love' way of life. I think she will be good at looking after my dog when I am away on business. I think he will be able to make a good Sunday roast. I think she will understand my need for recreational drugs. Finally somebody that I can share long walks with, that I can have anal sex with, that I can learn line-dancing with, that I can bring along to our company Christmas parties, that I can go on colonic irrigation retreats with, that I can compete for Triathlons with, that I can take cooking classes with, that I can go on survival treks in the Gobi dessert with. I think he/she will complete me, will be faithful to me, will protect me, will be kind-hearted, will be generous, will be supportive, and will make me happy.

Having a long wishing list is completely normal and a natural part of being a human being who would like a partner that they can share their life with. The long list of needs however, doesn't stop during the initial courtship. And it can be difficult to notice when we carry on applying our conditioned emotional references when we have settled in to our relationships. So as this wish list is founded in non-love and therefore based on people-pleasing and the belief that love equals mutual satisfaction of needs, then you eventually come across the 'If you really loved me, then you would ……. phenomena' further down the maturing relationship:

"If you really loved me then you would want to spend Christmas with my family". "If you really loved me, then you would understand that I need a little cannabis every day". "If you really loved me, then you would understand that as you don't want to put on the Bat Girl costume for me that I need to spend time with somebody that does now and then". "If you really loved me, then you would love my cat too". "If you really loved me, then you would stay at home with me every day until my broken leg has healed". "If you really loved me, then you would want to dress up in black latex for me and smack my bottom with a fly-swatter whilst I play the flute". "If you really loved me, then you would be happy for me when I go trekking for six months alone". "If you really loved me, then you would read this book that I am raving about so that we can share the experience". "If you really loved me, then you would make chicken soup for me when I have a cold - just like my mother did because she loved me" etc.

When we feel that our beloved looks, sounds and smells right - we are only half way there. When we feel that we love somebody for all sorts of reasons or for no reason at all - we are only half way there. When we feel that our beloved is our Soulmate or Twinsoul - we are only half way there. Embracing the act of loving denotes that we are not capable of truly loving somebody until we relinquish any attempt to fabricate even the tiniest story, or assumption, or fantasy about our beloved. We are not able to love anybody until we know our beloved for all that he or she is. – It is not about knowing enough for **you** to be satisfied that you are capable of loving them. It is not about being able to love everything about them to include, their shady past, smelly feet, nose picking in front of the television, farting in bed, tendency to leave breadcrumbs in the butter and grumpy demeanor in the morning; as well as their cute smile, their beautiful singing voice, their strong arms, their magic ways with children, their fabulous cooking skills and dog/horse/fish-whispering abilities. It is about knowing everything that they are passionate about, everything that they believe, all their wants and needs, all their dislikes and loathes **and especially why**. It is especially about knowing what motivates them – for example: Are they helping everybody in your neighborhood with the grocery shopping because it makes them feel good, because they want people to like them, because it keeps their mind busy so that they don't have to think about their own problems, because your neighbors cannot do it themselves and have nobody else in the whole world to help them, or for an entirely different reason? It is about knowing enough about your beloved to truly honouring them by seeing, hearing and sensing them for all that they are. More importantly, it is about catching yourself when you are about to interpret what they say or do into something they are not actually saying or doing. And most importantly, it is about resisting fabricating even the tiniest little story about them to satisfy your own needs and desires as you develop together each day.

Sadly you often see couples, who are struggling in failing relationships that are being advised to spice up their sex-life by playing role-play and trying out "new things" which can only take them further away from Love. If they made an effort to really honour each other instead then they would find out if they are capable of really loving each other, or if they are only able to care for each other. Then they could decide to split up and embrace new possibilities for experiencing Love, instead of merely using each other as another human body to be in close proximity to in order to avoid feeling lonely. There are plenty of people who are fully capable of honouring and thereby truly loving each other but who settle with "50% love" relationships where every day is about fitting in life around each other instead of making an effort and truly enjoy learning to really know each other: I do this; you do that. I take the kids to school; you pick them up after school. I know you don't like salt on your egg; you know I don't like milk in my porridge. I know you need a couple of hours in the morning before you feel like talking; you know I need quiet time after dinner. On Saturday we will take the kids out and experience something together; on Sunday we will then watch TV and play with our iPads, and so forth.

Some relationships have also been based on old myths, such as: "You should always leave a bit of mystery and not reveal everything about your self in a relationship", "Women are enigmatic creatures and simply impossible to understand", "Men just want a quiet life", "Dark, moody and mysterious men are really attractive" and "What you see is what you get". None of this belongs in the act of loving. If you do not show up in the relationship as the True You then Love falls flat in front of your feet; if we do not honour our beloved as their True Self then we are only able to offer them our biologically chemical, and spiritual experience combined with non-love; if our beloved does not show up in the relationship as their True Self then we will not know who to love. - If truth is absent from the relationship then we halt the flow of Love.

The act of loving is not about 'accepting' your beloved for all that they are; it is about 'honouring' your beloved for all that they are. When you accept a person for all that they are you are still motivated by your needs as there is an element of accommodating and tolerating in accepting another person. When you honour another person then you are motivated by Love. You may find down the road that you are only able to accept everything they are, or that you actually don't even like them after all – and that is perfectly ok. You may find down the road that you are only able to care for them and not able to love them after all - and that is perfectly ok. You do not **have to** love anybody on a personal level and nobody **has to** love you in this way – not even your parents; we just have to be honest about this so that we do not end up playing non-love games and therefore wasting our lives.

If your parents love you but will not honour the fact that you are gay – are you then really loved? Is it really you that they love?

If your parents love you but will not honour that you have chosen a different life to what they had envisaged for you – are you then truly loved? Is it really you that they love or do they merely love the fact that you are their daughter or son? Is that enough?

If your partner loves you but still sees you as the person they thought you were when you met – are you then really loved?

If your partner loves you but doesn't understand what you like, what you dislike, what makes your blood boil, what is important to you, what you believe in, what you are passionate about, what you want **and especially why** – are you then really loved?

If your partner loves you but blames you for behaving in a way that you do not – is it you that they love?

Where in your relationships are you motivated by non-love?

Where in your relationships are you motivated by Love?

Are you really seeing, hearing and sensing the people you love?

Do you really know all that you are? Do you really know what is motivating you?

Are you expressing and showing up in your life as all that you really are? Are you showing up in the world as the True You?

Is the True You being loved?

Meditation

I am standing in a small wooden temple by a calm lake surrounded entirely by white Camellia flowers. The temple is painted red and it is decorated with gold symbols. It is raining and the air feels soft and fresh and smells of ozone. You can also smell the earthy fragrance of the soil as it gets soaked by the rain. I step out into the rain and let the gentle rain drops fall on my face and body. When I look up I see that each rain drop is being transformed into white rose petals that float slowly and gently through the air. I stretch out my hands and let the rose petals fall on my face and into my hands. Falling, falling, gently and softly. White and soft. White and slowly. White and gently. I close my eyes with the knowing that I was born pure and that my heart is pure – now and always. I know that I was born loveable and I am loveable – now and always. I know that I was born free and I am free – now and always. I know that I was born strong and I am strong – now and always. I enjoy this pure, white, soft gentleness for as long as I want until I open my eyes, and I see that the soft white petals have been transformed into the purest white light. I am holding this pure white light, this pure Love - Love Absolute - in my hands and then I place it gently in my Heart Chakra. When I am ready, I take a deep breath and fill my body with the soft pure air and then I return to this other world – walking with pure light and pure Love in my Heart.

9. The Invitation to turn up the Volume on Love

I am fully aware that I have wasted more than 40 years of my life on participating in non-love and even endorsing anti-love during some of that time, and so I rejoiced when I came across a documentary, produced by CERN. The documentary is an inside story about the staff and associated scientists at CERN up to the announcement, on 4 July, 2012, of the discovery of the Higgs boson. [The Higgs boson is a sub atomic particle that is responsible for giving the rest of the particles in the universe mass – this is why it has also been nicknamed, The God Particle. Without it, our world would not be recognizable.] In the documentary you see various professors keeping each other company and exchanging their fears and hopes whilst waiting for the announcement. You overhear a discussion between Professor Ricardo Barbieri, Theoretical Physicist at Italy's Scvola Normale Superione di Pisa, and Savas Dimopoulis, Particle Physicist at Stanford University: Ricardo Barbieri says that he may be looking at having wasted 40 years of his life on nothing if it turns out that it is not the Higgs boson that has been discovered after all. Savas Dimopoulos replies that he would have wasted 30 years, and then he says: "But independently of that, you will know the truth". Wow!

The truth is that right now in this very moment, thousands upon thousands of children are being molested. In one camp we have the Non-Dualists saying that, that is just a divine event or an event that 'just is'. In another camp we have world religions that call it God's will and 'meant to be'. In another camp we have the outdated scientists that say that this is 'only human' and unavoidable as people are naturally bound to do bad things to each other, especially when we are over 7 billion earthlings trying to get along. I am suggesting that none of that is true.

The truth is that the entire world is creating the entire world in every second of the day. We are all contributing to the creation of this world. We are all the reason why good things happen and why evil things happen in every second of the day. The truth is that we are the creators of what is meant to be, and so what we thought was meant to be doesn't have to be. We are the ones that show up, act, react, hide, ignore, stand up, change channels, don't change channels, shout out, walk away, look on, get involved, and don't show up. Every thing that happens in this world happens because one or more human beings take action or choose inaction. Because we have believed that we were powerless and incapable of stopping anti-love, and because we allowed non-love to thrive instead of Love, we have wasted generation after generation, brain-washing each other into believing that suffering was meaningful and we forgot what it really meant to Love and be Loved.

The truth is that we are all incredibly strong and resilient. We are all born precious. You are precious. Your Life is precious. We are all unique. Even identical twins are not 100% identical. We all have something unique to bring to this world. The truth is that we are beautiful magical beings and we create magic on a daily basis. We create strange and rare illnesses with peculiar symptoms. We create globally unified illnesses and body ailments that a lot of people get, and we create people that never get the ailments that a lot of people get. We can fall out of airplanes and off mountain tops and still be here to tell the tale. We can finish each other's sentences and think of a person before they call us. We can emit and see aura. We can heal via Placebo Effect, Non-cebo Effect and spontaneous remission. We can make other people feel better just by showing up, holding their hand, and by listening and being fully present. We can create Peace by being Peace.

The truth is that Love is quite magnificent. Unlike energy, which can be loaded with positivity or negativity and then manifest as positive or negative outcomes, Love is different; Love is Love. Love cannot be loaded or infused with anything. You cannot blame anything on Love. We have all heard the old saying and sung along to, "Love hurts". The truth is that Love cannot hurt – it is the lack of Love and longing for Love that hurts. Love cannot cause anything else than Love. Love is continuously Love.

The truth is that human beings are great conductors of Love and we are fully equipped to share and exchange Love with each other – both on a human to human level, and on a deeply intimate and romantic level. We are the primary conductors of Love on this planet. And so I would like to invite you to, each day, embrace the True You. I would like to invite you to, each day, show up and share the True You with our world. I would like to invite you to, each day, follow your Heart instead of your hope. I would like to invite you to, each day, ask for the truth from the people you meet on your path. I would like to invite you to, right now, completely turn off your belief in the necessity of anti-love. I would like to invite you to, each day, turn down non-love more and more and more, until it is so, so very quiet that we can no longer feel or hear it. In other words, I would like to invite you to join me in turning up the volume on Love. And then I would like to invite you to turn the volume right up.

I do not believe in meaningful suffering.
I do not believe in an 'is-ness' in suffering.
I believe in Love.
I feel Love.
I know Love.
I absolutely know Love. That is all I truly know.
I see that actions based on Love nourish, rebuild and heal our world.
I believe in humanity's capacity, capability, ability and primal desire to Love.
I believe that the very essence of humanity is Love.
It is therefore I believe in the possibility of true Peace.
What do you choose to believe?

With Love,

♥HeleneMarie♥

Printed in Great Britain
by Amazon